# LONDON'S
## TRANSPORT RECALLED

**Half title page:** London was once the busiest port in the world, handling a rich variety of goods, with a vast network of docks located eastwards from Tower Bridge on both sides of the Thames. On 11 April 1964, Canadian Pacific's *Beaverash* (4,529GRT) off-loads its cargo in the Royal Victoria Dock (1855-1981). Built in Stockholm and launched as *Mimer* in 1958, she was owned by CP between 1963 and 1969. The Holland-America vessel in the background is the veteran *Dongedyk* (10,492GRT) of 1929. *(Ian Wells)*

# LONDON'S
## TRANSPORT RECALLED

### A PICTORIAL HISTORY

## MARTIN JENKINS & CHARLES ROBERTS

PEN & SWORD
**TRANSPORT**

AN IMPRINT OF PEN & SWORD BOOKS LTD.
YORKSHIRE – PHILADELPHIA

First published in Great Britain in 2019 by
Pen and Sword Transport
An imprint of
Pen & Sword Books Ltd
Yorkshire - Philadelphia

ISBN 978 1 52672 697 1

Typeset by Aura Technology and Software Services, India
Printed and bound in India by Replika Press Pvt. Ltd.

Pen & Sword Books Ltd incorporates the Imprints of Pen & Sword Books Archaeology, Atlas, Aviation, Battleground, Discovery, Family History, History, Maritime, Military, Naval, Politics, Railways, Select, Transport, True Crime, Fiction, Frontline Books, Leo Cooper, Praetorian Press, Seaforth Publishing, Wharncliffe and White Owl.

For a complete list of Pen & Sword titles please contact

PEN & SWORD BOOKS LIMITED
47 Church Street, Barnsley, South Yorkshire, S70 2AS, England
E-mail: enquiries@pen-and-sword.co.uk
Website: www.pen-and-sword.co.uk

or

PEN AND SWORD BOOKS
1950 Lawrence Rd, Havertown, PA 19083, USA
E-mail: Uspen-and-sword@casematepublishers.com
Website: www.penandswordbooks.com

# London's Transport Recalled

As authors we share a life-long fascination with the extraordinary range of all forms of transport to be found in and around London.

'My first visit was in 1947. We stayed near Kingston and I clearly remember being asked to alight from an elderly single-decker on the 213 so it could stagger up a particularly steep hill whilst we walked. At the top, everyone climbed back on board seemingly totally unperturbed. I also recall a PLA tour of the docks and crossing on the Woolwich Free Ferry on one of those magnificent paddle steamers. Between 1948 and 1951, I rode by tram to Purley and Woolwich and through the Kingsway Subway and then, in 1955, I visited the site of Penhall Road 'tramatorium' and managed to find several enamel running number plates (still treasured relics) in the undergrowth. In the late 1950s, I explored the entire trolleybus network with a series of Red Rover tickets. Later, I covered much of the local bus and rail network. For many years, I worked close to Oxford Circus which enabled me to observe the changing transport scene at close quarters. My first photographs were of trams on the Embankment (where else!) and Daimlers at Morden.' (Martin)

'My first exposures to transport in London were early childhood presents of books – Miroslav Šašek's whimsical illustrations of buses and the Underground in *This is London*, and the Ladybird Book *In the Train*, where the travellers have to cross the capital on their summer holiday. It wasn't long before I was able to experience the real thing for myself. A speedy journey to Euston just after electrification, the Tube to Waterloo, and a Southern Region emu to our final destination. On one day during the holiday, the grown-ups wanted to go shopping but I quickly made my excuses and happily spent time on the steps of Bentall's in Kingston (purely by coincidence!) watching the RFs and RTs go by. Railway trips of the 1970s acquainted me with the main line stations and loco depots – Finsbury Park, Stratford, Hither Green, Old Oak Common and the rest. The 1980s found me working for LT's bus division, including a spell driving the 9s and 27s out of Stamford Brook and sightseeing from the cab of my Routemaster – Albert Hall, Hyde Park Corner, Piccadilly Circus, Trafalgar Square, Fleet Street, etc. I retain a fascination for the city and its ever-changing transport scene.' (Charles)

For several years, we have been actively engaged in unearthing and conserving rare colour slides and negatives, some of which are now over 70 years old. For this book, nearly all our selected images mainly date from the period 1949 to 1969 and cover traffic on the Thames: canals, docks, ships, tugs, bridges and ferries; buses, trams, trolleybuses, depots and garages; railways, stations, locomotive sheds and freight yards; the Underground in all its facets; central area streets, suburbs, gas works, industrial premises and scrapyards; street furniture, fashions and buildings, as well as 'hidden gems' such as the Post Office Railway and the world's only double-decker tram subway. Most have never been published before and were taken by dedicated photographers, each of whom had the foresight to record things that were set to disappear during the years covered by this book. As authors, we owe them a huge debt and hope this colourful kaleidoscope will ignite memories of the rich complexity of former transport delights that could be seen in and around London.

One image has given us both considerable pleasure. It depicts a grimy dockland coal yard with an elderly horse attached to a cart just before setting off to make deliveries to houses in and around Poplar. The view encapsulates the dying days of the horse age as well as the London of smoke and smog before implementation of the Clean Air Act.

Because there have been so many books devoted to the historical aspects of the different forms of transport, ours is not a history book although we have included limited information in some of the captions. The views are all taken within the confines of the area once served by red and green London Transport buses. Our aim has been to show as many of the different classes of bus, tram and trolleybus which operated during the years 1949-69 although a few have eluded us. Starting in the central area, we follow a flexible geographic journey using the spoke-like pattern of the main railway lines as a framework. You never quite know what is round the next corner – or on the next page. We hope this will be a journey of surprises.

# Acknowledgements

We should like to thank all the photographers who have contributed to this book. We also wish to thank Robin Fell of The Transport Treasury, Michael Wickham for access to his collection and David Brown and Nicholas Britton for undertaking detailed scanning work. Also Nigel Bowker, John Laker, Alan Murray, Hugh Taylor, David Ventry and Ian Wells for checking our captions. As with the authors' other transport-related books, this volume has been compiled in conjunction with Online Transport Archive (OTA), a UK registered charity dedicated to the preservation and conservation of transport images and to which the authors' fees have been donated. For further detailed information about the archive, please contact the Secretary at 25 Monkmoor Road, Shrewsbury, SY2 5AG (email secretary@onlinetransportarchive.org).

**On its formation in** 1933, London Transport (LT) inherited a mixed fleet of some 2,600 tramcars. Conversion to trolleybus began shortly afterwards and would have been completed in the 1940s if the war had not intervened. As a result, replacement of the remaining trams did not begin until 1950. Some will still recall the distinctive sight and sound of these first generation trams. On a quiet morning in August 1950, E/1 1770 crosses Westminster Bridge. Rehabilitated in 1936, this is one of a group of cars (1727-1776) built by Hurst Nelson in 1922. Route 26 was replaced by buses two months later and 1770 withdrawn shortly afterwards. (*Copyright Michael Wickham*)

**'Goodbye old tram'** –
**this** quote from the
tramway film *The Elephant
Will Never Forget* captures
the emotion of the final
day. Just 13 hours later, Big
Ben would toll the passing
of an era as thousands
of Londoners bid 'au
revoir' to their trams.
(*Photographer unknown*)

**Heading west from
Trafalgar** Square on route 9
to Mortlake garage is RTL434.
It is from the fleet of 1,631
7ft 6in wide Leyland PD2s
delivered during 1948-54, all
of which had Leyland engines,
AEC transmission and 56-seat
bodies supplied by three
manufacturers. After becoming
a staff bus in 1966, this example
was sold in 1970. (*Fred Ivey*)

**This stunning overview of** Piccadilly Circus dates from July 1949. Leading the trio of buses emerging from Shaftesbury Avenue is a three-axle LT-class followed by an RT and behind them – complete with London Transport roundel on the radiator – one of 170 new ECW-bodied Bristol Ks diverted to the capital in the late 1940s. After helping to overcome a severe shortage, all had departed by September 1950. (*Copyright Michael Wickham*)

**Shortly before withdrawal, LT271** rounds Trafalgar Square in April 1949. It is one of over 1,220 LT (**L**ong **T**ype) three-axle AEC Renown 663s delivered between 1929 and 1932 with 56- or 60-seat bodies built by several manufacturers. This one had a petrol engine and pre-selective gearbox and was based at Plumstead garage. (*Copyright Michael Wickham*)

**For decades, Londoners enjoyed** sailing on pleasure craft to destinations such as Margate and Southend. One of the last vessels involved in this once-lucrative trade was MV *Royal Sovereign* (1.950GRT). Built by William Denny for the General Steam Navigation Company in 1949, this well-appointed ship is seen at Tower Pier on 7 July 1965. With passenger numbers plummeting, GSN ended sailings in 1966 after which she was converted into a Cross-Channel lorry transporter and renamed *Autocarrier*. (*Phil Tatt/Online Transport Archive*)

**Crossing Tower Bridge in** October 1967 is RTL1432. Although nominally dating from 1953, the system of body and chassis swapping which was employed during the overhaul process meant that a vehicle displaying a particular number was usually totally different from the one which did so when the vehicle was new. (*Alan Mortimer/Online Transport Archive*)

**A party of excited** school children prepare to explore the sights round Buckingham Palace in July 1963. Among the row of coaches is one of the short wheelbase 'private hire' RFs delivered in 1951. (*Copyright Michael Wickham*)

**St Paul's dominates the** skyline in this 1957 view of the River Lighterage Company's *Brent Brook* towing six coal barges to feed the furnaces of a riverside power station or gas works. Built by Henry Scarr of Hessle, she remained on the Thames until the bulk movement of coal fell into decline and was sold in 1971. (*Marcus Eavis/Online Transport Archive*)

**Heading upstream in 1968** is *Croydon,* a flatiron collier belonging to the South Eastern Gas Board. Built by the Burntisland Shipbuilding Co. in 1951, it transported coal to various gas works until the UK decided to convert to natural gas, after which the vessel was sold in 1971. (*Marcus Eavis/Online Transport Archive*)

13

**Large crowds saw the** brand new TSS *Dover* (3,602GRT) visit the Pool of London on 7 July 1965. This roll-on, roll-off car ferry was the last steam ship built for British Railways and the first to carry this new Sealink livery. Launched on the Tyne by Swan, Hunter and Wigham Richardson, she was renamed in 1978 and sold three years later. For centuries the Pool was at the heart of London's commercial activity. (*Phil Tatt/Online Transport Archive*)

Sister GSN vessel to the *Royal Sovereign*, the MV *Royal Daffodil* (2,060GRT, 1939) had been requisitioned for military service during the Second World War and was involved in the Dunkirk evacuation. Post-war, she settled down to a programme of Thames cruises and Cross-Channel trips until scrapped in 1967. She is seen here in 1964. (*Phil Tatt/Online Transport Archive*)

During a Soviet Exhibition held in August 1968, trips were offered on board *Kometa*, one of the Soviets' sleek hydrofoils, at £1 per head. (*Marcus Eavis/Online Transport Archive*).

**The nearest trams came** to the major tourist sites was the Embankment loop accessed from either Blackfriars or Westminster bridges. Most cars went right round but others terminated midway, whilst some plunged into the Kingsway Subway. By July 1952, only six quite long routes remained; for example, it would take Brush-built 343 of 1925 some 75 minutes to reach Abbey Wood. This is one of the former West Ham Corporation E/1s built between 1925 and 1931 with a variety of bodies and trucks as well as distinctive indicator displays and narrow upper deck advertising panels. Together with similar cars from Croydon, East Ham, Leyton, London County Council and Walthamstow, they were absorbed into the London Transport fleet in 1933. (*C. Carter/Online Transport Archive*)

**Heading along the Embankment** towards
Westminster Bridge in May 1955 is RT248. This is
from the massive fleet of nearly 4,700 RTs delivered
between 1947 and 1954. All were AEC Regent IIIs
with elegant 56-seat bodies mostly by Park Royal and
Weymann but also Cravens and Saunders, withdrawals
taking place between 1955 and 1979. This one has
a roofbox Park Royal body and was withdrawn in
1963. Formerly a heavily-trafficked tram corridor,
the Embankment is today almost bereft of buses.
(*Copyright Michael Wickham*)

**London boasted the only** double-deck tram
subway in the world. Linking Bloomsbury to the
Embankment, it had subterranean stations at Holborn
and Aldwych. When opened in 1906, it was worked
by single-deckers but after being deepened in 1931 it
became the preserve of metal-bodied E/3s. To prevent
two trams being on the same track at the same time
on the 1-in-10 gradient, movements were controlled
by electric light signals. This unique structure closed to
trams in April 1952. (*J. Law/Online Transport Archive*)

**At the north end** of Blackfriars Bridge, the tram tracks were on the west side and the conduit slot off-centre. Heading away from the Embankment in 1950 is one of the Brush-bodied E/1s (81-100) delivered to East Ham Corporation during 1927/8. Distinguished by their small upper-deck route number boxes, they spent their post-war life at Abbey Wood depot. (*Photographer unknown/G.E. Lloyd collection, courtesy Martin Jenkins/ Online Transport Archive*)

**The effects of the** bombing close to Southwark Bridge are clearly visible in this view dating from July 1952. Waiting to depart is No. 2 – latterly the only 'oddity' in the London tram fleet. Following an accident, E/1 1370 was rebuilt into this domed-roof car in 1935. On much of the surviving post-war system, the trams drew their power from a conduit slot between the rails and not from the more conventional overhead wires. (*G.W. Morant collection/Online Transport Archive*)

**Several trolleybus routes terminated** just inside the City of London. Turning towards its layover point in Charterhouse Street in 1958 is JI 920. This is from a group of AECs with Weymann bodies (905-951) delivered in 1938, most of which were withdrawn in April 1960. (*Marcus Eavis/Online Transport Archive*)

**London's trolleybus network was** once the largest in the world, its web of wires spreading over much of the area north of the Thames. However, as with the trams, most inner termini were simply too far from the central area. In 1961, all-Leyland K1 No. 1301 negotiates the Tottenham Court Road terminal loop. Plans to extend the wires towards New Oxford Street encountered strong opposition. (*John Ryan*)

**Many workers arriving by** trolleybus at Moorgate could walk into the City. Waiting to leave for Hampstead Heath in 1960 is M1 1552, one of a small batch of unit construction AECs (1530-1554) with Weymann bodies featuring more streamlined upper deck fronts. (*Marcus Eavis/ Online Transport Archive*)

**Several trolleybus routes passed** close to King's Cross and St Pancras Stations. Working an outbound 613 to Parliament Hill Fields is C1 159. Looking somewhat weary by 1954, it belongs to a batch of AECs (132-183) delivered in 1935 with a mix of Weymann and Metro-Cammell 70-seat bodies, this being one of the latter. Note the handsome rear mudguards, known to enthusiasts as 'spats'. The C1s were all withdrawn by 1955, with five seeing further service in Malaya. (*Ian Stewart Collection/Online Transport Archive*)

**Whitehall has always been** a busy transport corridor. One of a group of Duple-bodied Daimlers (D132-181) with 'Relaxed Utility' style bodies, D163 is en route to Tooting in 1951. Initially assigned to Green Line duties at Romford in 1946, they ended their days at Merton or Sutton garages as red Central Area buses. (*W.J. Wyse/LRTA (London Area)/Online Transport Archive*)

**Emerging from Whitehall on** 31 August 1968 is RT4804 which is carrying a Saunders roof-box body. New in 1954, it lasted until late 1969 after which it was sold. It is carrying a side/rear blind at the front in place of the usual via blind, and its under-canopy route number box is not functioning. (*W. Ryan*)

**In this action scene,** a police officer on point-duty holds back traffic on Whitehall, including two NS type buses and an early taxicab. Introduced in 1924, the NS was the last major class to feature open-tops, exposed driving positions and solid tyres. Later NSs did incorporate modern features and some earlier examples were subsequently retrofitted. Although the last NS ran in 1937, route 11 still uses Whitehall. (*Claude Freise-Green,* The Open-Road, *1926*)

**Oxford Street was lavishly** decorated for the Coronation of HM Queen Elizabeth II in June 1953. The westbound convoy of buses is headed by one of 281 Daimler Utility buses delivered during 1944 and 1946 with AEC engines and bodies supplied by various manufacturers. At this time, cars were allowed to park in the middle of the carriageway. (*Copyright Michael Wickham*)

**In this view of** Baker Street, RCL2228 is working the seasonal 726 to Whipsnade Zoo which was permanently withdrawn in September 1968. It is one of 43 longer Routemaster coaches dating from 1965 which had powerful AEC engines, 65-seat Park Royal bodies with folding doors, luggage racks, comfy seats and fluorescent lighting. They also had deeper style front wings with no cut outs for ventilator grilles or spotlights. (*John Herting/Online Transport Archive*)

**The Metropolitan Railway received** twenty Bo-Bo electric locomotives from Metropolitan-Vickers of Barrow in 1922/3. One fascinating freight working involved coal deliveries to and refuse collection from Chiltern Court, the railway-owned apartment block above Baker Street Underground station. No. 2 *Thomas Lord* is seen on this duty shortly before it ended on 3 August 1961. (*Harry Luff/Online Transport Archive*)

**London's earliest underground railway** was the cut and cover section from Paddington to Farringdon which opened in 1863 and now forms part of the Circle Line. By 1876, it extended eastwards through Liverpool Street, where a P Stock train arrives with an Aldgate service on 22 May 1956. Waiting in the headshunt ready to move forward to haul a Metropolitan Line train is Bo-Bo electric No. 12 *Sarah Siddons*. (*R.E. Vincent/The Transport Library*)

**On a Sunday morning,** RTW35 turns into Victoria Street at the start of its journey to Hampstead Heath. Some of the newspapers available in the 1950s have since ceased publication and most of the buildings, including the impressive Duke of York pub, have been demolished. (*Copyright Michael Wickham*)

*Opposite below:*
**Victoria was one of** the termini for the first of a planned network of 'express' bus routes, the 500 being introduced in April 1966. Marketed as 'Red Arrow', these limited stop services provided fast links between main line stations and key business and commercial districts. At first, six experimental rear-engined AEC Merlins with 36ft long Strachan bodies were used. These had front entrance, twin turnstiles, centre exit, 25 seats and space for 48 standees. XMS2 was photographed on 22 April 1966. (*R.L. Wilson/Online Transport Archive*)

LT operated such a highly-standardised fleet that any unusual buses always attracted attention. One such vehicle was FRM1. Built as a joint venture between LT, AEC and Park Royal, it was the only rear-engined, front loading Routemaster. Shortly after entering service in June 1967, it suffered a fire which led to the provision of opening windows, as seen here at Victoria on 1 September 1968. This one-off passed to the LT Museum in 1984. (*W. Ryan*)

**Passing the Royal Fusiliers**
War Memorial in Holborn is RML3 (later RM3), the last of a quartet of experimental Routemasters to be delivered. Fitted with a Leyland engine, its Weymann body had a different style of bonnet and wings from production RMs. Few will recall this bus as it was only in passenger use from January 1958 to October 1959, after which it served in the training fleet until 1972. (*Basil Hancock collection*)

**On a quiet Sunday** morning in 1958, RTW300 passes under the imposing Holborn Viaduct. (*Julian Thompson/Online Transport Archive*)

*Opposite above:*
**Unknown to many Londoners** was another underground railway owned and operated by the Post Office. Opened in 1927, this 2ft gauge line served various sorting offices between Paddington and Whitechapel. The mail-carrying trains were driverless and operated at 440V dc third rail. The original trains were replaced in the 1930s by the English Electric stock seen here. The line closed in 2003 but a short section has reopened as part of the Postal Museum. (*John Herting/Online Transport Archive*)

**Rounding Parliament Square in** August 1966 is XA17, one of 50 Leyland Atlanteans (XA1-50) with 72-seat Park Royal bodies, the first of which appeared the previous year on route 24. Following comparison trials with Routemasters and Daimler Fleetlines, these buses were deemed unsuited for London and sold to the China Motor Bus Company in 1973. (*Alan Mortimer/Online Transport Archive*)

**In 1965, eight experimental** Daimler Fleetlines (XF1-8) with 72-seat Park Royal bodies were delivered to East Grinstead garage. In 1966, they were exchanged for several months for comparison trials with eight Central Area Leyland Atlanteans and XF2 is seen during this period at Moorgate on route 272. All of LT's green buses passed to London Country Bus Services (LCBS) in 1970, with which these Fleetlines survived until 1981. (*C. Carter/ Online Transport Archive*)

Amongst a throng of buses at Charing Cross in 1953 is RT1514, one of the RT type to have five-window bodies supplied by Cravens of Sheffield between 1948 and 1950. This view highlights the pronounced curve to the rear upper deck. Being non-standard, these 'Cravens' (RT1402-1521) were disposed of in 1956/7. Alongside are two RTWs with their fleet numbers painted on the rear dome, a peculiarity of Upton Park garage. All are in the 1946 red and cream livery. (Copyright Michael Wickham)

Broad Street Station provides the backdrop for two 'Red Arrow' AEC Merlins with 36ft long MCCW bodies. They are working the 502 introduced in September 1968. Note the white on blue express destination blind. The 650 production Merlins introduced in 1968/9 had various configurations of doors and seating depending on the work they were intended for. 'Red Arrow' Merlins were two-door, 25-seat, 48-standee and designated MBA. (C. Carter/Online Transport Archive)

**Euston is one of** the major rail termini fringing Central London. Although retaining an impressive frontage, the platforms and train sheds were dilapidated by the 1960s. Complete with headboard, 'Duchess' 46255 *City of Hereford* backs down onto the stock for the down 'Caledonian' to Glasgow. These powerful 4-6-2 Pacifics were designed by Sir William Stanier for express passenger duties and lasted until the West Coast Main line (WCML) was electrified. (*Kevin McCormack Collection*)

**Between 1961 and 1966,** the station underwent a major redevelopment in preparation for electric services, resulting in the demolition of the famous arch and hotel. The new order is illustrated by AM10 four-car emu 050, departing with a semi-fast service to Coventry, nicely framed by Bo-Bo electrics in their original Electric Blue livery with cast aluminium lion insignia. (*Phil Tatt/Online Transport Archive*)

**In steam days, motive** power depots (MPDs) provided coaling, servicing and maintenance facilities for both passenger, freight and shunting locos. Camden MPD was noted for handling main line engines working in and out of Euston. 'Duchess' 46245 *City of London* rests on shed on 1 August 1963, showing the attractive maroon livery carried by some members of this class to good effect. The loco was withdrawn as part of the final cull of the class in September 1964. (*Kevin McCormack Collection*)

**'Rebuilt Patriot' 45530** *Sir Frank Ree* heads north past the labyrinth of tunnels and dive-unders at Primrose Hill in the summer sunlight on 10 June 1963 with the 7.15pm Euston-Northampton train. (*Charles Firminger/Online Transport Archive*)

**In 1962, RTW279 is** at the layover point for route 31 in Camden Town. These 8ft wide buses were initially banned from streets served by trams and from Central Area routes until tests showed that wider buses were acceptable. (*Tony Belton*)

**Offset by elegant houses** on Harrington Square, RTW484 and RT3375 head south in 1958. (*Julian Thompson/Online Transport Archive*)

**A Standard Eight overtakes** L3 class 1383 as it climbs leafy Camden Road towards its junction with Holloway Road. The heavily-used U-shaped 653 was worked by trolleybuses between March 1939 and January 1961. The white ring on the traction pole indicated the presence of a feeder providing electricity to the overhead wires. (*R.E. Vincent/The Transport Library*)

**An up mixed freight,** headed by Stanier 8F 48362, passes through South Kenton on the slow lines on 8 June 1962. (*Charles Firminger/Online Transport Archive*)

**Filled with football fans** at Wembley in 1962 is RF6, one of the twenty-five short 27ft 6in RFs (1-25) delivered in time for the 1951 Festival of Britain, their 35-seat Metro-Cammell bodies having glazed roof panels for excursion and private hire work. The bus is in an unusual all-over green livery, with fleet name and number in red. All were withdrawn during 1962/3. (*Fred Ivey*)

**Heading towards Sudbury with** the destination already reset for the return to Paddington on 10 April 1959 is 288, one of 100 C3 class trolleybuses with BRCW bodies (284-383) delivered during 1936/7. The last examples were withdrawn later in the year. (*John A. Clarke*)

**One of the first** 'standard' LT 70-seat, three-axle trolleybuses, No. 262, is seen on the Harrow Road. It is from a group of 100 C2 Class with Metro-Cammell bodies (184-283) and 80hp motors delivered in 1936. (*R.E. Vincent/The Transport Library*)

*Opposite below:*
**North of Queens Park,** Bakerloo Line trains ran on tracks then owned by BR. Until 1982, some went through to Watford but most terminated at Harrow and Wealdstone. In the late 1960s, a train of 1938 Tube Stock stands in the headshunt at Harrow before starting its southbound journey. (*Ron Copson/Online Transport Archive*)

In an attempt to reduce costs, BR introduced some experimental four-wheel railbuses in 1953. These could operate in two- or three-car formation. A mixed set (note the different opening window designs) departs from Harrow and Wealdstone in May 1955 with a service on the branch to Belmont. Known as 'Flying Bricks' they lasted until 1959 and the Belmont branch until 1964. (*Ray DeGroote/Online Transport Archive*)

WARNING
KEEP OFF
ELECTRIC
LIVE RAILS

PASSENGERS MUST
CROSS THE LINE
BY THE BRIDGE

**In June 1969, RLH74** is about to pass beneath the low bridge carrying the Belmont Branch over Christchurch Avenue, Harrow. Operated by Central Area RLHs since 1952, the 230 was about to be converted to flat-fare, OMO single-deckers. All 76 RLHs were 'provincial' style AEC Regent III with lowbridge 53-seat Weymann bodies, with RLH53-76 being initially assigned to the Central Area. (*Alan Mortimer/ Online Transport Archive*)

**Between Harrow and Watford** is a six-track layout featuring the fast and slow lines of the WCML and the fourth-rail electrified lines used by local services out of Euston. On 29 April 1962, Stanier 'Jubilee' 4-6-0 45552 *Silver Jubilee* heads towards Euston with the 5.35am from Preston. (*Charles Firminger/Online Transport Archive*)

**The six-track layout can** be clearly seen in this picture of 'Princess Royal' Class Pacific 46204 *Princess Louise* as it powers towards the capital with a rake of coaches in red and cream livery approaching Headstone Lane. (*Neil Davenport/Online Transport Archive*)

**By 9 May 1964,** electrification gantries have been erected, but are awaiting wiring. By now, steam on the WCML had largely been replaced by diesel power. Here, split headcode box English Electric Type 4 D331 on an up express overtakes Type 1 D8007 on a semi-fast working. (*Douglas Twizzell/ The Transport Library*)

Watford Junction remains the stop closest to Euston for some WCML express trains. In 1966, AL6 Type electric (later Class 86) E3111 works the 10.13am Birmingham New Street to Euston. (*Marcus Eavis/ Online Transport Archive*)

For many years, three-car dc electric units built in 1957/8 were the preserve of stopping services from Euston to Watford. They also worked the branch to Croxley Green and one is seen at this terminus whilst working the shuttle to Watford Junction on 28 August 1963. The last of these units were withdrawn in 1985 and services to Croxley Green ceased in 1996. (*John Ryan*)

In 1956, LT opened the world's largest bus overhaul works at Aldenham on the site of an unfinished underground depot adapted during the war to build aircraft. As it was in a remote location, most of the workforce was bussed in so each evening an exodus of staff buses departed for far-flung destinations. Leading this convoy is RT329 bound for Tring. The works closed in 1986. (*John Herting/Online Transport Archive*)

**Passing Garston garage on** the 727 is RC9, one of fourteen coaches (RC1-14) intended to improve flagging Green Line fortunes. When delivered in 1965, these AEC Reliances had 36ft long dual-purpose 49-seat Willowbrook bodies, although in 1969 some had their seating reduced and luggage racks installed for working the prestigious inter-airport 727. The last were withdrawn from the LCBS training fleet in 1979. (*John Herting/Online Transport Archive*)

**Seen in Hemel Hempstead** in February 1969 is RMC1508 on the 708 to East Grinstead. This is from the group of Routemaster coaches (RMC1453-1520) delivered in 1962 to replace RFs on some Green Line services. Fitted with twin headlamps, platform doors, fluorescent lighting and no external advertisements, these 57-seaters failed to generate additional traffic especially when battling congestion and competing rail services. All passed to London Country in 1970, most ending their days as ordinary buses. (*Alan Mortimer/Online Transport Archive*)

**The semi-rural 387 linked** Tring village to its railway station and to farming communities at Aldbury. RF588 is from a large group of underfloor engined AEC Regal IVs (RF514-700) which were assigned to the Country Area in 1953/4. All had 30ft long, 41-seat MCCW bodies with platform doors, a welcome addition in wintery weather. The last green RFs were withdrawn by LCBS in 1978. (*John Herting/Online Transport Archive*)

Due in no small part to John Betjeman, the Poet Laureate, St Pancras escaped the fate of Euston and retained its ornate façade, which now forms part of the International terminus. For many years former Midland Railway 4-4-0s were the mainstay of express passenger workings. In this rare picture, taken in 1948 shortly after nationalisation, 40182 retains its LMS designation but has received its BR number. (*C. Carter, © TfL from The London Transport Museum Collection*)

**Seen on Chichele Road,** Cricklewood, is E1 class 564. It is from a batch of AECs with Brush bodies (554-603) delivered during 1937. Apart from D2 class 483, these were the first trolleybuses to have full bulkheads, most earlier classes being subsequently rebuilt. (*Peter Grace/John Laker Collection*)

**Steam workings were in** the process of being supplanted by the time Type 4 D84 heads the 6.33pm St Pancras-Derby service past Welsh Harp Junction signalbox, near Cricklewoood, on 12 May 1961, in the days before locos were given yellow front warning panels. (*Charles Firminger/ Online Transport Archive*)

**Photographed at Dunstable in** the late 1950s is T790, one of a batch of 15T13 'provincial' AEC Regal IIIs (T769-798) delivered in 1948 with 31-seat front-loading Mann Egerton bodies. All were withdrawn by 1962, although a couple survived as staff buses until 1963. *(Peter Jones collection)*

**King's Cross is arguably** London's most prestigious terminus. From here, crack expresses depart on the East Coast Main Line (ECML) for York, Newcastle, Edinburgh and beyond. In this late 1950s view, generally disobeying the warning sign, trainspotters young and old gather to watch the departure of an A2 Class Pacific with a rake of mixed coaching stock. (*Julian Thompson/Online Transport Archive*)

**Arriving at King's Cross** with an up express is the world-famous Gresley Pacific 60022 *Mallard*. The crest showing it is holder of the world speed record for steam is clearly visible. Built 1935-8, the thirty-five A4 streamliners were the Eastern Region's flagship locomotives until relegated to less glamorous duties by the onset of dieselisation. The last A4s were withdrawn in 1966, although *Mallard* had been set aside for preservation two years earlier. *(W.J. Wyse/LRTA (London Area)/ Online Transport Archive)*

**Pristine locos awaiting their** next turn of duty could always be found at King's Cross 'Top Shed'. This is an A3 Pacific, one of Nigel Gresley's first three-cylinder express passenger engines. Though less celebrated than classmate *Flying Scotsman*, 60055 *Woolwinder* presents an impressive sight shortly after it had been fitted with a double chimney. It survived until 1961. *(Kevin McCormack Collection)*

**In the late 1960s,** Upminster & District 563 (formerly RTW413) poses against a run-down block of early flats at King's Cross. Note the mother calling down to her child from the fourth floor balcony. (*John Herting/Online Transport Archive*)

**Immediately north of King's** Cross are the Copenhagen Tunnels, from which Brush Type 2 D5678 is seen emerging in September 1961 with a rake of Pullman Coaches. Charging supplementary fares and with carriages in umber and cream livery, Pullman services were the epitome of high quality rail travel. (*R.E. Vincent/The Transport Library*)

In 1945, approximately 870 trams operated on 100 route miles of which 90 per cent was on the conduit. Only two truncated prongs still penetrated the northern trolleybus empire, one of which reached Archway where former LCC No. 1 is seen in April 1951. Dating from 1932, this technically-advanced tram was intended as the forerunner of a fleet of 100 new cars. It was sold to Leeds in 1951. (*Tom Marsh/Online Transport Archive*)

Trolleybuses tackling the 1-in-10 gradient on Highgate Hill were equipped with special coasting and run-back brakes. Between 1939 and 1960, the 611 (Moorgate-Highgate Village) was worked by J3 AECs (1030-1054) with BRCW bodies delivered in 1938 and chassisless Metro-Cammell L1s (1355-1369) delivered in 1939. L1 1362 (left) and J3 1053 are seen here in 1960. Cable and electric trams once climbed this fearsome grade. (*Marcus Eavis/Online Transport Archive*)

The 210 (Golders Green-Finsbury Park) was the first Central Area route to receive RFs in 1952. They remained for nearly 20 years although latterly OMO. Here RF421 is seen at hilly Hampstead Heath. (*John Herting/Online Transport Archive*)

**Passing the Hampstead Heath War Memorial** in 1969 is MB381. Delivered the previous year, this was one of a group of Central Area OMO single-door AEC Merlins (MB304-397) with 50-seat MCCW bodies. It was sold in 1977. (*John Herting/Online Transport Archive*)

**Used to replace steam** on the most important workings on the ECML were the 22 strong 'Deltic' Type 5 diesel-electrics introduced in 1961/2. Shortly before being named, D9005 speeds through Hornsey with an up express in 1963. (*Julian Thompson/Online Transport Archive*)

**In steam days, many** stopping services on the ECML were in the hands of LNER four-car sets of 'Quad-Art' coaches. Their articulated characteristics can clearly be seen in this view taken on 12 June 1953 at Hadley Wood, where the combination is led by ex-LNER Gresley N2 0-6-2T 69589. Note the condensing apparatus allowing the locomotive to work the semi-underground 'Widened Lines' into Moorgate. (*J.B.C. McCann/Online Transport Archive*)

55

**Approaching Potters Bar from** the north with a Pullman service is Peppercorn A1 Pacific 60120 *Kittiwake*. Although ordered by the LNER from its Doncaster Works, the 48 production members of this class were not delivered until shortly after nationalisation. (*Julian Thompson/Online Transport Archive*)

*Opposite below:*
**Seen working the 240A** in Mill Hill in September 1962 is TD99, its 'lazy blind' showing both termini. It is one of the second batch of TD-class Leyland PS1s (TD32-131) with Mann Egerton bodies delivered during 1948/9, the last examples being withdrawn later in 1962. (*Fred Ivey*)

**Always a major attraction,** Ally Pally (Alexandra Palace) was served by route 233 which was converted to single-deck, flat-fare, OMO in September 1968 as route W3. A month earlier, RT1809 leaves for Finsbury Park Station. The box located on the front pillar was meant to accommodate the semaphore indicator signal but these were never fitted and the boxes were plated over. (*Alan Mortimer/Online Transport Archive.*)

**The Underground extended into** many of the northern suburbs through the transfer of lines from other companies. For example, the LNER's ex-Great Northern routes to High Barnet and Edgware (the latter truncated at Mill Hill East) were transferred to LT in 1940 and the main line origins of Finchley Central can be seen in this view. One train of 1938 Tube Stock is pictured en route to Morden, while another, on the far left, is about to use the single track branch to Mill Hill East. (*Marcus Eavis/Online Transport Archive*)

**Seen crossing the ECML** on Oakleigh Road North, Brunswick Park, is RF399, one of the red Central Area RFs (289-513) delivered during 1952/3. Unlike their Country cousins, they came originally without platform doors although some had them fitted later. The final red RFs lasted until 1979. (*Alan Mortimer/ Online Transport Archive*)

**Most of the main** trolleybus corridors had intense peak hour services. During a crew change outside Finchley trolleybus depot, the booms on L3 1457 have been lowered so that sister vehicle 1466 can pass carefully on the outside as it comes off service on a bitterly cold 2 January 1962. (*Tony Belton*)

**Shortly before being sold,** RT1314 worked the 114 during the summer of 1962. Seen at Edgware, it still has the small pillar-mounted route plates introduced in 1946, on which the digits were displayed vertically. The roof-mounted number boxes were dispensed with due, in part, to damage from tree foliage. (*Tony Belton*)

**Many longer LT routes** had short workings; for example, those boarding 1669 in Barnet will only be able to go as far as Islington Green. This is from a group of N2 class AECs (1645-1669) with Park Royal bodies noted for their rounded front ends and thick corner pillars. This view was taken after displaced N2s had been allocated to Finchley depot in April 1960. *(Ian Stewart/Online Transport Archive)*

**Waiting to leave Enfield** in 1961 is 1062, one of 300 all-Leyland Ks (1055-1354) delivered during 1938/9. This is a K1 with Metrovick motors and controllers. Brown paint was applied to the rear domes to disguise the grease dripping from the collector shoes. *(Mike Skeggs)*

**One of the less** significant terminal stations was Broad Street. Opened in 1865, it was mostly used by suburban services to east and west London. Some of these lines were electrified in 1922 and were still worked by this original 'Oerlikon' stock in May 1949. Note the early post-nationalisation livery with 'British Railways' designation. These units were gone by 1960 and an increasingly neglected Broad Street finally succumbed in 1986. (*R.E. Vincent/The Transport Library*)

**Dalston Junction was where** the branch to Broad Street connected with the main North London Line. Some services to the east were diesel operated. This photograph shows the transition period between the original green livery and the new Rail Blue. High density, Derby-built units such as these were familiar sights around London well into the 1980s. (*Marcus Eavis/ Online Transport Archive*)

**Station pilots at Liverpool** Street were kept in pristine condition. In the late 1950s, N7 0-6-2T 69614 is stabled in a centre road between shunting duties. It was in stock until 1960. These engines were also regulars on Liverpool Street's many suburban services. Note the large piles of parcels on the adjacent platform, recalling the days when such traffic was a significant source of revenue. (*W.J. Wyse/ LRTA (London Area)/Online Transport Archive*)

**An early nationalisation scene** at Liverpool Street. Both locomotives have BR numbers but retain LNER-style liveries. On the left is Gresley-designed B17 4-6-0 'Footballer' 61665 *Leicester City* – note the metallic football integrated into the nameplate – whilst alongside is 61258, one of the ubiquitous B1 4-6-0s first introduced in 1942. (*R.E. Vincent/The Transport Library*)

**Change came to Liverpool**
Street in 1949 when services to Shenfield were electrified at 1500V dc. Subsequent electrification was at 6.25kV ac (later 25kV ac). This included the line to Clacton for which AM9 Class units, capable of 100mph running, were built in 1963. They were the only class of emu ever to carry BR maroon livery. (*Phil Tatt/ Online Transport Archive*)

**In 1947, LNER 'Rebuilt Sandringham'**
B2 4-6-0 1671 *Royal Sovereign* in apple green livery heads a train of teak-bodied stock past the site of the short-lived Bishopsgate (Low Level) station (1875-1916). Between 1946 and 1958, this locomotive was designated for use on Royal Trains to and from Wolferton, for Sandringham House. (*R.E. Vincent/The Transport Library*)

**Prior to the electrification** of the Chingford branch in 1960, an unidentified 0-6-2 tank engine coasts towards the terminal station with a 'Quint-Art' set of articulated coaches. The hoarding publicises construction of a carriage washing plant as part of the 1955 BR Modernisation Plan. (*Julian Thompson/Online Transport Archive*)

**Shortly before its withdrawal,** ST816 rests outside the Royal Forest Hotel in Chingford on 26 March 1949. It is one of over 1,100 ST (**S**hort **T**ype) AEC Regent 661s built mostly for the LGOC in 1929-32 but with a range of different bodies. Also on view are a green ST and a Utility Guy. On summer Sundays, the 38 was extended into Epping Forest, a popular destination for thousands of Londoners. (*C. Carter, © TfL from the London Transport Museum Collection*)

**Seen in Buckhurst Hill** on 3 June 1950 is STD165, one of 65 all-Leyland PD1s purchased in 1946 to replace life-expired vehicles. Route 20 was one of their regular haunts. Following service cuts in 1955, STD112-176 were sold to Yugoslavia. (*C. Carter, © TfL from the London Transport Museum Collection*)

**Post-electrification, the Chingford Branch** was operated by AM5 Type three-car emus. Carrying Rail Blue livery with full yellow ends, unit 420 is leaving Walthamstow Central en route to Chingford in August 1968. (*C. Carter/Online Transport Archive*)

**Passing the Greyhound Stadium** on Chingford Road, Walthamstow, is RML2266. Although the stadium closed in 2008, the Grade II listed façade survives. This bus was in stock from 1965 to 2005. (*John Herting/Online Transport Archive*)

**In September 1968, bus** routes in Walthamstow were reorganised to act as feeders to the new Victoria Line. They met with limited success. Seen in Stainforth Road on newly-created circular W21 is MBS201, one of 76 two-door OMO MCCW bodied AEC Merlins (MBS194-269). Designed for suburban flat fare routes, these 36 footers proved difficult to manoeuvre and expensive to overhaul, this one being sold in 1977. (*C. Carter/Online Transport Archive*)

**Stamford Hill once hummed** with trolleybuses. As well as being a regular terminus, it was also an intermediary point on the long run to Waltham Cross. 1691 is an all-Leyland K3 (1672-1696) delivered in late 1940. (*Marcus Eavis/ Online Transport Archive*)

**Waltham Cross was the** mostly northerly point served by trolleybuses. The all-conquering Routemaster had ousted trolleybuses on the 627, 659 and 679 in April 1961 and the 649 would succumb in the July. Eking out its final days is 1678, one of a small group of all-Leyland K3s delivered during 1940. Possibly the passenger is challenging the duty inspector about the wisdom of dispensing with electric traction! (*Marcus Eavis/Online Transport Archive*)

**Leading three RTs along** Lea Bridge Road on extended trolleybus replacement route 257 is RM212. Note the gas holder and the absence of high rise buildings. (*R.E. Vincent/The Transport Library*)

**London's canals had once** played a vital role in the economy. Even into the late 1950s, the last vestiges of horse propulsion could still be found. Here, a bargee leads his charge past the lock-keeper's cottage at Tottenham Lock on the River Lee Navigation, with the *Vandyke* safely moored in the chamber. (*Julian Thompson/Online Transport Archive*)

71

A **wealth of vehicles** was on view at Hertford Bus Station in 1951. The first of five views shows STL996. This was one of 139 Country area STLs built in the mid-1930s with 52-seat bodies, their doorless front entrances leading to complaints about draughts. The second picture is of C50, a Leyland Cub with a 20-seat Short Bros. body. Out of the 106 C-class one-man Cubs delivered during the mid-1930s, 74 were assigned to the Country Area for lightly-trafficked routes. All had gone by 1954. The third scene shows Q215. This is one of 50 AEC 6Q6 Green Line coaches (Q189-238) delivered in 1936/7 with centre-entrance, 32-seat Park Royal bodies, mass withdrawals taking place during 1952. A mixed bag of 238 Qs were delivered, all with offside engines. The network of Green Line coach services was established by the LGOC in 1930 and the fourth view shows T599, one of a group of 10T10 coaches (T453-748) delivered during 1938/9. These AEC Regal IVs had front-loading Chiswick-built bodies with this one surviving until early 1954. The final image is of STL2683, one of the short-lived post-war STLs (2682-2701) with provincial-style Weymann bodies delivered in 1946. All were sold in 1955. (*Copyright Michael Wickham (STL2683); Alan B. Cross collection (others)*)

**In 1949, the former** Great Eastern Railway (GER) line north of Loughton was transferred to LT. However, the replacement Central Line electric service only ran as far as Epping which left the section to Ongar still steam-worked on LT's behalf by BR. When finally electrified in 1957, Epping-Ongar generally remained a shuttle until closure in 1994. This three-car set of mid-1920s Standard Stock is seen at Ongar on 28 April 1962. (*Charles Firminger/Online Transport Archive*)

**The rural stretch of** the Central Line between Woodford and Hainault was used to trial automatic train operation (ATO) before its full-scale introduction on the Victoria Line. In the first scene, a set of 1960 Tube Stock emerges from Grange Hill Tunnel. This Stock consisted of twelve Driving Motor cars supplied by Cravens of Sheffield, which were initially matched up with Standard Stock trailers – note the different profiles in this train – to form four-car sets. The last of these trains ran in 1994. The second view shows a set of 1967 Stock – its rounded ends distinguishing it from previous designs – pulling into Hainault on test. (*Marcus Eavis/Online Transport Archive; Ron Copson/Online Transport Archive*)

**Among routes serving the** industrial complexes at Dagenham was the 145 to Chingford. Shortly before it was withdrawn in August 1949, LT322 is seen on Woodford Avenue near Claybury Broadway. The last LTs survived until early 1950. The second view depicts G316, one of the 435 Guys delivered between 1942 and 1946 with various Gardner engines and basic Utility bodies. In service from 1945 to 1953, this Arab II has a Massey body. The brown and cream-liveried vehicle in the background is a Leyland PD1 from the City Coach Company on their Wood Green to Southend service. (*R.E. Vincent/The Transport Library*)

**Carrying an advert for** the now defunct airline TWA, RM194 passes the Crown and Crooked Billet, Woodford Bridge, in August 1968. Introduced in April 1960, the 275 was one of those routes extended beyond the limits of the former trolleybus wiring (route 625). The bus was sold to Sri Lanka in 1988. (*Alan Mortimer/Online Transport Archive*)

**Barkingside was one of** the places served by 43 trolleybuses destined for Durban and Johannesburg but allocated to LT during the war. Special dispensation was needed to operate these 8ft wide vehicles, which were based at Ilford depot, for local routes 691 and 693. Sub-divided according to electrical equipment, the 25 Durban Leyland SA1s (1722-1733) and SA2s (1734-1746) had 72-seat Metro-Cammell bodies with panelled over sliding doors at the front, large indicators and tinted upper deck windows. The last survivors were withdrawn in 1959, including 1723 seen here. (*Frank Hunt/LRTA London Area/ Online Transport Archive*)

**Rounding the corner at** East Street, Barking, is 1763, one of the 18 AECs SA3 (1747-1764) ordered by Johannesburg. This view clearly shows the panelled over jack-knife front exit, the Jo'burg style indicators and the rounded nature of the 72-seat Metro-Cammell body. Although LT once planned to keep routes 691 and 693 until 1962, both closed in August 1959. (*Julian Thompson/Online Transport Archive*)

**Passenger rail closures in** the London area have been relatively rare. One casualty was the former GER branch to Palace Gates, which closed in early 1963 because of its proximity to Wood Green on the ECML and LT's Piccadilly Line. In September 1962, Darlington-built L1 2-6-4 tank engine 67729 simmers at intermediate station West Green. (*Roy Hobbs/Online Transport Archive*)

**From 1840, a massive** site in Stratford was developed as a labour-intensive railway works and motive power depot. This mid-1950s overview gives some idea of the on-site activities. In the foreground, two small tank engines are on shunting duty, whilst to the right is a collection of new diesel shunters in their black livery. (*G.E. Lloyd Collection, courtesy Martin Jenkins/Online Transport Archive*)

*Opposite below:*
**Preparing to oust steam** from local services, Cravens-built diesel multiple units were delivered to the ER in 1958. Two-car set E51267/E56425 enters Stratford after a spell of driver training on the Lea Valley Line. (*Marcus Eavis/Online Transport Archive*)

**Until the early 1960s,** Stratford remained a major overhaul works for Eastern Region (ER) locomotives. Gresley K3 61942 is newly outshopped in 1957, with an equally pristine N7 69666 behind it. The entire site was subsequently bulldozed and is now occupied by Stratford International station and a large shopping complex. (*G.E. Lloyd Collection, courtesy Martin Jenkins/ Online Transport Archive*)

**Areas close to the** docks suffered heavily during the war. Sixty-one trolleybuses were so badly damaged by enemy action that they received new bodies from different manufacturers. Included was E1 578C, the suffix C indicating Northern Coachbuilders. Shortly before withdrawal in 1959, it is turning into aptly-named Tramway Avenue, Stratford. (*Phil Tatt/Online Transport Archive*)

**Seen at Leyton Green** on 4 April 1959 is K2 class 1339. This is from the large group of vehicles (1155-1254/1305-1354) delivered during 1938/9. As the conversion programme bit deeper, some of these sturdy all-Leylands migrated west and survived to the end. As passenger loadings declined in the 1950s, service levels on the 555 had been gradually reduced. It ran for the last time some ten days later. (*John A. Clarke*)

**Stratford is bedevilled by** low railway bridges, some of which had 5mph speed restrictions for drivers on the 178 to Clapton, being operated here by RLH64. When withdrawn in April 1971, this was the last route using this class of bus. (*Phil Tatt/Online Transport Archive*)

**In its heyday, London** was the busiest port in the world, handling a rich variety of goods. To allow commerce to flourish, wharfs, docks and quays covered much of the north bank of the Thames east of London Bridge. The Fred Olsen vessel *Bergerac* (3,607GRT) of 1955 is probably discharging a perishable cargo. Note the wealth of activity on the quayside. The wharf ceased to be used in 1970. (*Doris Davenport/Online Transport Archive*)

**For many years, the** short East London line was a somewhat gloomy affair. When opened in 1869, it made use of a former Brunel pedestrian tunnel (1843) under the Thames. By the time this view was taken at Whitechapel, it was electrified and formed part of the Underground network. Characterised by their elliptical front windows, F Stock, nicknamed 'Tanks', had been introduced by the District Railway in 1920 and ran until 1963. (*Frank Hunt/ LRTA (London Area)/Online Transport Archive*)

**As the trolleybus turning** circle at London Docks was so tight, movements were only meant to take place under supervision but this rarely happened. Overlooked by the impregnable wall of the dock estate, K2 1326 leaves the loading point on Dock Street heading for Gardiner's Corner in early 1961, whilst the driver of the next 647 is on full lock as he negotiates the circle. (*John Ryan*)

**An excellent overview of** Gardiner's Corner, once London's busiest trolleybus junction where some 4,000 vehicles a day clicked through the 'cat's cradle' of overhead wires, equal to a trolleybus every ten seconds in rush hours. (*Julian Thompson/Online Transport Archive*)

**One of several connections** between the Thames and London's canal system is Regents Canal Dock at Limehouse. Here, a group of lighters, including *Croydon* and *Autumn*, enter from the river in September 1965. Today, the dock is given over to leisure use and the viaduct in the background carries the DLR (Docklands Light Railway). (*J.G. Parkinson/Online Transport Archive*)

**Among oddities dotting the** dock estate was this unique four-wheel battery electric loco built by the Midland Railway in 1913 to shunt a busy coal yard adjacent to West India Dock station. Oddly, this was not physically connected to the rail network, wagons being lowered and raised via an hydraulic hoist. This was also used to extract BEL No. 1 when it went away for maintenance. The yard closed in 1964 but the Thornfield House flats in the background are still standing. (*Harry Luff/Online Transport Archive*)

**One stop on the** Railway Enthusiasts' Club 'East London Rail Tour' of 26 August 1961 was deep in dockland at Millwall Junction. Ex-LMS Ivatt 2-6-0 46472 is seen on the Blackwall exchange lines with the Port of London Authority (PLA) network, the dockside cranes providing an impressive backdrop. Today this railway scene has vanished, replaced by the DLR and a busy dual carriageway. (*John Ryan*)

*Opposite below:*
**By the 1960s, demand** for domestic coal had almost disappeared, due in part to the Clean Air Act, which was intended to prevent deaths caused by 'killer smogs'. Most remaining onward deliveries from the yard were by lorry, but H. Underdown were still using a traditional horse-drawn dray. Their animal was believed to be 17 years old. (*Harry Luff/Online Transport Archive*)

**These views of West** India Docks feature two German-built vessels requisitioned by the British and then sold to Hellenic Lines. In the first view, *Rodopi* (1,923GRT) has an export cargo including new Land Rovers on 3 June 1972. Launched at Lübeck in 1944, she is a standard wartime German 'Hansa A' type freighter. The second view depicts *Patrai* (2,754GRT) one of the larger, wartime 'Hansa B' freighters which was launched at Flensburg in 1947, having been incomplete when captured. The two vessels were scrapped in 1974 and 1984 respectively. The first West India Dock dated from 1802. Although investment had occurred in the 1970s, increasing containerisation led to closure in 1980. (*Ian Wells; Nigel Bowker*)

**Tugs played a vital** role in assisting vessels to and from moorings and through various locks. Seen in West India are two of the PLA's post-war fleet of diesel-powered tugs, *Platina* (1952) and *Plagal* (1951), which were built by Henry Scarr of Hessle. In the background is *London Samson* (1,075GRT). Built in Holland and equipped with diesel-electric machinery, this floating crane was acquired by the PLA in 1963 and sold in 1991. (*Nigel Bowker*)

*Opposite below:*
**At Bromley-by-Bow, heading for** Fenchurch Street under the wires with the 12.25pm from Tilbury on 7 April 1962, is Fairburn 2-6-4 tank engine 42227. Though an LMS design, this class continued to be built by BR until 1951. Note the period cars and lorries and further examples of prefab housing. The latter were mass produced after the war to provide much-needed accommodation for those made homeless during the blitz. (*Charles Firminger/Online Transport Archive*)

**Flanked by the former** Essoldo cinema, RTL75 has just turned off East India Dock Road, Poplar, in 1967. This was from the first batch of 118 Park Royal RTLs which entered service in 1948, most of which were disposed of following the 1958 bus strike. However, this one survived until 1969. Note the Bedford TK lorry heading to the docks and the prefab housing. (*John Herting/Online Transport Archive*)

**Some early locos survived** for many years. One such was 58857, a powerful but compact 0-6-0T engine built in 1888 by the North London Railway at its Bow Works. Seen only a few miles from its birthplace, it waits at Poplar for its next shunting duty. It was withdrawn in April 1958. (*G.E. Lloyd Collection, courtesy Martin Jenkins/Online Transport Archive*)

**Another venerable survivor was** ex-GER J15 (formerly Y14) 65361, dating from 1888. Although other members of the class were withdrawn as early as 1920, this is still going strong on 7 April 1962 as it passes through Abbey Gate near West Ham with a short dockland freight train. This 0-6-0 would be withdrawn for scrap five months later. (*Charles Firminger/Online Transport Archive*)

This view of the former West Ham Corporation tram depot was taken on 26 April 1960. For over 20 years, it was home to the E2 (604-628) and E3 (629-653) class AEC trolleybuses delivered during 1936/7. Although the latter had all gone by 1956, most of the Weymann-bodied E2s survived until early 1960 with 622 outlasting all the others so it could enter the history books as the first and last trolleybus to operate from the depot. (*John Buckle*)

**When Royal Victoria Dock** opened, London was still the first port of Empire with thousands employed in and around the massive dock estate. Berthed on the north side on 18 August 1962 are two post-war refrigerated Blue Star freighters, each with limited passenger accommodation. *Uruguay Star* (10,723GRT) was launched by Cammell, Laird in 1948 and *Wellington Star* (11,994GRT) by John Brown in 1952. The former was sold for scrap in 1972 and the latter in 1976, although it survived until 1979. (*Ian Wells*)

**This view taken on** 30 July 1962 shows the sheer bulk of the giant flour mills that once occupied the south side of Royal Victoria. Formerly owned by Spillers and Rank Hovis, some sections are still standing. (*Ian Wells*)

**To shunt the docks** on the north side of the Thames, the PLA maintained a large fleet of locomotives with those serving the Royal Docks being stabled mostly near Custom House on the exchange sidings at Royal Victoria Dock. The engines seen here in 1970 were from a large group of 0-6-0 diesels supplied by the Yorkshire Engine Company in 1956-9, which ousted the last of the steam locos. (*Marcus Eavis/Online Transport Archive*)

**Negotiating Customs House terminal** loop in June 1969 is RM104 which entered service some ten years earlier in November 1959. The bus has an early body with non-opening front upper-deck windows. (*Alan Mortimer/Online Transport Archive*)

**Among routes serving North** Woolwich were the busy 101, which paralleled the Royal Albert Dock, and the 669 which had been extended beyond the limits of the trams it replaced. In 1959, Saunders-bodied RT1288 passes 969, one of a group of BRCW-bodied AEC J2s (955-1029) delivered in 1938. 300 RT bodies were built in 1950/51 by the Anglesey-based Saunders, when the normal suppliers were unable to keep up with the rate of chassis deliveries. (*Phil Tatt/Online Transport Archive*)

**Guided by a pair** of Sun tugs, MV *Irish Sycamore* (10,560GRT) is manoeuvring in Royal Albert Dock (1880) on 29 September 1962, having brought grain from New Orleans, destined for Spillers Mill. Owned by Irish Shipping Ltd., she was built in Hartlepool in 1961 and scrapped 1984. (*Ian Wells*)

**A powerful study of** SS *Ocean Cock* (182GRT) in Royal Albert on 8 June 1962. Owned by Gamecock Tugs Ltd., she was built in Aberdeen in 1932 and took part in the Dunkirk evacuation before being requisitioned. She was later converted to oil-burning and broken up in 1969. (*Ian Wells*)

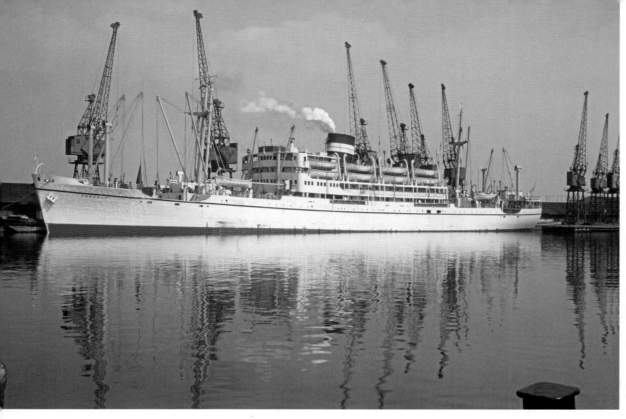

**Loading in Royal Albert** Dock on 1 September 1962 is MV *Sangola* (8,645GRT). Built in Glasgow in 1947 for the British India Steam Navigation Company, this cargo/passenger freighter was broken up in April 1963, so this was one of her final voyages. (*Ian Wells*)

**Designed to handle the** largest steamships, King George V Dock (1921-81) was only operational for 60 years. Berthed on the north side on 18 August 1962 is *Glengyle*. Launched by Caledon Shipbuilding and Engineering Co. of Dundee in 1939, one of eight similar cargo liners, she was requisitioned prior to delivery and returned to Glen Line in 1946 after a distinguished war career. Sold in 1970, she was scrapped the following year. (*Ian Wells*)

**Built originally for the** meat and tobacco trade, there was still plenty of activity in Royal Albert Dock in 1971. On view are *Baltistan* (7,489GRT – Strick Line, 1953), *Benvrackie* (9,757GRT – Ben Line, 1955) and *Plankton* (160GRT) built for the PLA in 1965. The tug survived until sold in 1991 but the two general cargo freighters were gone by the mid-1970s. This dock closed in 1980. (*Marcus Eavis/ Online Transport Archive*)

**The North Thames Gas** Board works at Beckton was the biggest in the world and was famous amongst enthusiasts for its long-lived steam locomotives. These worked on two levels shunting coal wagons to and from river jetties. No. 11 is an 0-4-0T engine built by Neilson and Company of Glasgow in 1879 and rebuilt locally in 1928. It was still going strong in 1959 but scrapped in 1961. The works closed in 1970. (*Charles Firminger/Online Transport Archive*)

**Thirty-two four-car AM7 units** were delivered the ER in 1956 for the electrification of the line from Liverpool Street to Southend Victoria. This unusual shot taken at Ilford shows unit 05s – the suffix standing for 'Southend' – with an experimental partial yellow end. As Class 307, these units remained on the line until the early 1990s, with some seeing further service in Yorkshire. (*Frank Hunt/ LRTA London Region/Online Transport Archive*)

**On a snowy day** in January 1965, an early Metro-Cammell dmu pulls into Purfleet with a Barking-Grays service to pick up a solitary, windswept passenger. (*Phil Tatt/Online Transport Archive*)

**58038 was the last** survivor of a batch of thirty 0-4-4T engines built for the Midland Railway in 1875/6. Shortly after nationalisation, it was photographed at Romford awaiting departure with a three-coach train for Upminster. The loco was scrapped in 1954. (*R. E. Vincent/The Transport Library*)

**Upminster town centre has** changed little since RLH69 was photographed on 4 May 1968. This was one of a handful of RLHs based at Hornchurch garage between 1955 and 1970 for working the short 248. (*W. Ryan*)

**Samuel Williams and Sons** had a range of interests around Dagenham Dock, including lighterage, barge building and repairing, as well as providing contract shunting for many of the industrial tenants on the site. Amongst locomotives employed was No. 4, an 1877-built Manning Wardle 0-6-0ST which was bought by Williams in 1889 and still in use in 1959 before being preserved. (*R.E. Vincent/The Transport Library*)

**Over the years, ships** were both built and broken up on the Thames. On 26 April 1964, two recently withdrawn Danish-built freighters, *Aguante* (1926) and *Parita* (1920), were beached at Thomas Ward's yard at Grays. Each had complex histories and, only months before, had arrived laden with cargo. (*Ian Wells*)

**Standing outside the gates** of the Mobil Oil refinery at Coryton is RT3242, which carries a Weymann body, in 1968. It passed to London Country and was withdrawn by them in 1972. (*John Herting/ Online Transport Archive*)

**Although Tilbury's first dock** opened in 1886, later investment saw it transformed into a significant container port, complete with deep-water moorings. As the outdated upstream docks declined, Tilbury grew in importance. Seen on 13 April 1963 is Ellerman Lines *City of Auckland* (7,713GRT). Built by Vickers-Armstrong, Newcastle in 1958 she was sold in 1978 and broken up in 1983. (*Ian Wells*)

**Among various vessels operated** on the railway-owned Tilbury-Gravesend ferry were two vehicle ferries ordered by the LMS from the Lytham Shipbuilding and Engineering Company in the mid-1920s. One of these – *Tessa* – is seen leaving Gravesend. Following the arrival of new motor vessels coupled with a sharp downturn in traffic, she was withdrawn in 1964. On the left is MV *Royal Daffodil*. (*Phil Tatt/Online Transport Archive*)

**Pictures of fireless steam** locomotives in action are comparatively rare. The Reed Paper Group operated a series of mills on the North Kent coast, with the Imperial Mill at Gravesend being one of two to use fireless engines, one of which is seen here on 17 August 1968. Rail traffic on the site ceased in about 1978 and the mill was closed three years later. (*John Ryan*)

**The 490 was one** of the Gravesend routes worked from Northfleet garage by members of the GS-class. This view of GS36 was taken in June 1967. Based on the Guy Vixen, these vehicles had 26-seat ECW bodies, Perkins diesel engines and normal control, and proved ideal for lightly trafficked one-man routes or for tackling difficult terrain such as the North Downs. (*John Herting/Online Transport Archive*)

**Working the 480 on** Galley Hill Road, Northfleet, in 1967 is RML2323, one of the first green RMLs to enter service in late 1965. Green Routemasters passed to London Country in 1970 but most passed back to LT in 1977-80, with whom they had extended lives. RML2323 lasted until 2004 and is now preserved. (*John Herting/Online Transport Archive*)

*Nevasa* **had a chequered** history. Built under government specification as a troopship for the British India Steam Navigation Company in 1956, loss of Empire, demise of National Service and the end of troop movements by sea led to her conversion into an educational cruise ship in the mid-1960s. However, soaring oil prices meant she became too expensive and these voyages ended in 1974. (*Nigel Bowker*)

*Opposite below:*
**In April 1964, RF156** leaves Wrotham in Kent for Amersham in Buckinghamshire. As loadings on the Green Line network haemorrhaged at an alarming rate, OMO was gradually introduced during the 1960s. (*Alan Mortimer/Online Transport Archive*)

**When the Dartford Road** Tunnel opened in August 1963 specially-designed buses were provided to transport cyclists. TT1-5 had Ford Thames Trader chassis and Strachan bodies with bike racks downstairs and seats upstairs. The loss-making service ended in October 1965. (*Alan Mortimer/Online Transport Archive*)

*Opposite above:*
**Much of the area** south of the Thames is served by a vast fan of lines electrified on the third rail. Over the years, these have been worked by a variety of stock designed for fast, semi-fast and stopping services. Seen departing from Erith on 11 March 1961 with the 2.12pm service from Charing Cross to Gravesend is 4-EPB unit 5048. First introduced in 1951, these high-capacity units operated right across the Southern Region's electrified network until the last examples were withdrawn in 1995. (*Charles Firminger/Online Transport Archive*)

**At their Erith Works,** British Insulated Callender's Cables operated a 3ft 6in internal railway to move cable drums for export to wharves on the Thames. Photographed in late 1967 is No. 3/3 *Woto*, built by Bagnall of Stafford in 1924, the unusual name being inspired by the Christian names of two members of the Callender family: William Octavius and Thomas Octavius. By this time, the engine was oil-fired – note the large tank on the footplate. (*Phil Tatt/Online Transport Archive*)

**Also in Erith, British** Oil and Cake Mills had a works producing edible oils and animal feedstuffs ('cake' being a protein supplement fed to cattle). A small fleet of locomotives shunted the site, including *Sir Vincent*, a 1917 0-4-0 built by Aveling and Porter of Rochester, better known for their steam traction engines, from which this design was derived. It is seen here on 11 March 1961 and ran until 1966 when replaced by a diesel and sold into preservation. (*Charles Firminger/Online Transport Archive*)

**British Portland Cement Manufacturers** utilised a line electrified at 250V to connect its Johnson's Works in Greenhithe with a pier on the Thames. Three unusual electric hopper wagons were supplied by English Electric in 1928 and these impressive machines survived until the end of electric operation, being scrapped in 1972. (*Harry Luff/Online Transport Archive*)

**In trolleybus days, Bexleyheath** was a busy junction with intense peak hour headways on routes 696 and 698. These linked Woolwich to Erith, Welling and Dartford. Seen shortly before withdrawal, 471 is one of the D2 Leylands (385-483) with Metro-Cammell bodies and Metro-Vick equipment delivered during 1936/7. (*Alan Watkins/Online Transport Archive*)

**Welling High Street was** among places served by trolleybuses housed at Bexleyheath depot. Seen in March 1959 is 798, one of 150 H1 Leylands with Metro-Cammell bodies (755-904) delivered in 1938, the bulk of which were withdrawn during 1960. (*John Buckle*)

**Eighty bus variants of** the Q (Q106-185) type were delivered in 1936, of which 53 were delivered in red for the Central Area. Q163 began life as a Country Area bus but is seen here at Sidcup in Central Area red. It survived until 1953. (*W.J. Wyse/LRTA (London Area)/ Online Transport Archive*)

**The section from Woolwich** to Abbey Wood was one of those where trams took power from overhead wires. In October 1949, 1182 is seen on McLeod Road. This is one of 1,000 wooden-bodied E/1s delivered between 1907 and 1912, all with maximum traction trucks. Over the years, many of these 70-seaters were upgraded and those surviving the war received driver's windscreens. 1182 was scrapped in 1951. Note the parallel trolleybus wires erected in 1935. (*W.E. Robertson*)

**Photographed at Eltham Church** on 21 April 1951 is E/1 312, one of the mixed bag of ex-West Ham Corporation cars, most of which lasted to the end. Built variously between 1925 and 1931, they had a variety of bodies and trucks as well as distinctive indicator displays. Note the difference in width of the upper deck advertising panel compared to the following car. (*C. Carter, © TfL from The London Transport Museum Collection*)

**Seen in the background** is the busy conduit change pit in the middle of Woolwich High Street. In peak hours, queues of cars would sometimes build up on either side. In August 1950, E/3 1957 is inbound for the Embankment. This is from the final batch of 100 trams (1904-2003) ordered by the LCC with Hurst Nelson bodies and EMB maximum-traction bogies. Most were in service from 1931 to 1952. Coming up on the inside is H/1 class trolleybus 796 making for its terminal point in Woolwich. (*C. Carter/Online Transport Archive*)

**From its introduction by** London County Council (LCC) in 1889, Woolwich Free Ferry was operated for over 70 years by twin-engined coal-fired paddle steamers of which the last four were delivered from Samuel White between 1922 and 1930. These side-loaders could carry 1,000 people but just 15-20 vehicles, so long queues often formed. They were replaced by diesel-engined motor vessels during 1963/4. (*Phil Tatt/Online Transport Archive*)

**Two views of Penhall** Road 'Tramatorium'. Dating from 1949, this was specially built to dispose of redundant trams and buses, the noxious smoke from the burning bodies leading to complaints. The first view taken on 8 September 1951 shows 2153, one of the 90 'Felthams' which escaped the inferno and was sold to Leeds together with LCC 'Bluebird' No. 1. E/1 1231, cut down to act as a site office, was not so lucky nor was pre-war, forward-entrance London Country STL970. (*C. Carter/ Online Transport Archive; W.J. Wyse/LRTA (London Area)/Online Transport Archive*)

**Dating from 1922, N** Class 2-6-0, 31817, pulls into Blackheath station with a down stopping train in May 1961. This is one of some 75 mixed traffic locos first introduced by the South Eastern and Chatham Railway (SE&CR) in 1917. Note the different liveries in the rake of coaches. (*Charles Firminger/ Online Transport Archive*)

**Seen near Blackwall Point** Power Station in August 1968, the small cargo vessel *Woodlark* (933GRT) was built for the General Steam Navigation Co. at Grangemouth Dockyard in 1956. She was sold to the MoD in 1969 and scrapped ten years later. (*Nigel Bowker*)

**Catford was once a** thriving tramway hub; for example, peak loadings on route 54 (Grove Park-Victoria) required some 40 trams. At the rear of this line-up on Bromley Road on 8 September 1951 is Brush-built 1514, one of over 150 E/1s rehabilitated during the mid-1930s with improved lighting and destination displays, comfortable seats, flush-side panels and driver's vestibules. Some survived until early 1952. (*C. Carter/Online Transport Archive*)

**Passing through Catford Bridge** on 8 September 1951 is No. 138, one of a batch of HR/2s (101-159) which had no trolleys and were therefore confined to conduit-only routes. Built by Hurst Nelson in 1931, they had four motors, EMB equal wheel bogies and special brakes for working on Dog Kennel Hill. All had gone by April 1952. (*C. Carter/Online Transport Archive*)

**St John's, the location** of a major accident in 1957, is seen here some four years later on 6 May 1961 with ex-SE&CR D1 Class 31739 powering through on the 7.24am London Bridge to Ramsgate service. It is from a group of some 700 similar 4-4-0 locomotives first introduced in 1921. Steam was withdrawn from these Southern Region (SR) services with the completion of the Kent Coast electrification scheme in 1961. (*Charles Firminger/Online Transport Archive*)

**London's last big tram** depot, with space for 314 cars on 32 tracks, was at New Cross. During crew changes, cars would line up outside. The last six routes still required 150 trams. By August 1952, some 2,000 tram drivers had retrained on buses. 169 is one of fifty English Electric bodied E/3s (161-210) purchased by Leyton Council in 1931. (*G.W. Morant collection/Online Transport Archive*)

Cresting the bridge at New Cross Station on 20 August 1950 is 2050, one of the fast but noisy former Walthamstow Corporation E/1s (2042-2053, Hurst Nelson 1927; 2054-2061, Brush 1932). Equipped with powerful motors, these 'Rockets' could pace a Feltham. (*C. Carter/Online Transport Archive*)

**A rare view of** PS *Queen of the South* (formerly *Jeanie Deans*, 1931) on one of the few occasions she actually managed to operate an advertised excursion from Tower Pier during the 1966/7 seasons. After ending her days on the Clyde, she had been purchased by enthusiasts and moved to the Thames. Despite considerable investment, she kept failing and went for scrap in December 1967. (*Harry Luff/Online Transport Archive*)

**The Queen and the** Duke of Edinburgh returned to Britain after a six-month long tour of the Commonwealth on 15 May 1954 aboard the Royal Yacht *Britannia* (John Brown and Co., 1953, 5,769GRT), which had only been commissioned a few months earlier. Also on board were Prince Charles, Princess Anne and Sir Winston Churchill. Hundreds of thousands watched the yacht's stately progress to Tower Pier. Here she rounds the Isle of Dogs. (*J.B.C. McCann/Online Transport Archive*)

**The Q Stock designation** was applied to a variety of modernised and new build District Line stock, some dating back to 1923, which could be formed into mixed sets. For example, this four-car unit seen leaving Surrey Docks (the present day Surrey Quays) station on the East London Line is headed by three older clerestory-roofed cars with a Q38 car at the back, differentiated by its flared-skirted body. (*Ron Copson/Online Transport Archive*)

It is hard to imagine the tonnage that once passed through the London docks, many of which had special facilities for specific cargoes. For example, the Surrey Docks complex had in the region of fourteen yards for handling imported timber. However, with no rail access, onward transhipment was by lighter or lorry. Framed in Canada Dock on 8 June 1962 is *Basil II, a* US Liberty ship launched in 1945 as *Allen G. Collins,* during the period she was registered under the Liberian flag. She was deemed a total loss after running aground in 1965. (*Ian Wells*)

Londoners flocked to explore any fighting vessels opened to the public. Flying the flag in Albion Dock in April 1970 are two early post-war diesel-electric Amphion or 'A' class submarines – *Acheron* and *Andrew.* The latter was the first British submarine to make a submerged crossing of the Atlantic, the last to have an on-deck gun and the last built to a World War II design. It was withdrawn in 1977 and *Acheron* five years earlier. (*Marcus Eavis/Online Transport Archive*)

In November 1965, RTW360 turns from Streatham Road into Southcroft Road just months before the last of this class were withdrawn in May 1966. Subsequently, 130 joined the driver training fleet and 279 were sold to Ceylon. (*Alan Mortimer/Online Transport Archive*)

*Opposite above:*
**This line-up of 'leaning-back'** STLs was taken outside Telford Avenue depot in 1948. At the front is STL570, one of a large batch (STL203-552/559-608) built at Chiswick during 1933/4. Following withdrawal in 1953, it joined the driver training fleet for two years. Note the differences in liveries, destination displays and lower-deck window arrangements. Despite many variations, the STL (**S**hort **T**ype **L**engthened) was in effect London's standard double-decker of the 1930s with hundreds of chassis being delivered by AEC between 1932 and 1939, most with diesel engines. (*Jack Law/Online Transport Archive*)

**This view of Gresham** Road, Brixton, shows one of the tramway change pits once located in the middle of the road. This was where trams changed from conduit to overhead and vice-versa, the plough-shifters armed with their plough forks only being protected by bollards and red flags. Latterly, some 800 men were needed to maintain the ageing conduit. (*W.E. Robertson*)

**During a lengthy bus** strike in 1958, the People's League for the Defence of Freedom operated seven free routes, although fares were charged after a couple of weeks. Among the strike-breaking vehicles was this former Leicester Corporation AEC Renown with a 64-seat MCW body. As a result of the strike, LT abandoned some routes and reduced headways on many others. (*W.J. Wyse/LRTA (London Area)/Online Transport Archive*)

**Working a tram replacement** route in Forest Hill is RTL299. When taken into stock in 1949, it had a Park Royal body. It survived until 1969. Note the Morris Minor Post Office Telephones van. (*John Herting/Online Transport Archive*)

**With its four parallel** tracks, Dog Kennel Hill was a tramway landmark. Following an early runaway, two additional tracks were built so four trams could be on the 1-in-11 grade at the same time. Latterly, only HR/2s ('**H**illy **R**outes') were used as each axle on the equal wheel trucks was motored. This view dates from October 1949. (*W.E. Robertson*)

**Elephant and Castle was** one of the busiest post-war tram junctions. In May 1950, E/1 1836 is seen en route to Wimbledon. Withdrawn in August 1951, it is from a group of E/1s (1777-1851) built by Brush in 1922 and mounted on Hurst Nelson bogies. Latterly, some cars had their wooden bodies strengthened by external bracing. (*C. Carter/Online Transport Archive*)

**In the middle of** this line-up at Elephant and Castle on 11 November 1950 is 2069, one of the 100 'Felthams' built by the UCC during 1930/1, of which 54 went to the Metropolitan Electric Tramways and 46 to London United. On passing to LT, they became 2066-2119 and 2120-2165 respectively. Designed for efficient passenger flow, they had front exits, all metal bodies, separate driver's cabs, straight staircases, no internal bulkheads, comfortable seats for 64 plus space for 20 standees, air brakes, EMB maximum traction trucks and body-mounted plough carriers. They also had heaters – very welcome in the cold and damp. (*C. Carter, © TfL from The London Transport Museum Collection*)

**London Bridge station has** through platforms for services to and from Charing Cross and Cannon Street as well as some terminal platforms. Seen at the latter on 23 June 1957 is former Southern Railway N15X Class 4-6-0 32331 *Beattie* which is providing traction for 'The Riverside Special' railtour. This locomotive was withdrawn the following month. (*Photographer unknown/John Pigott Collection*)

**The through platform section** of the station in 1958 sees 2-HAL unit 2615 with an up working and 4-EPB 5017 displaying a headcode for a Cannon Street to Gravesend or Maidstone West service. Always suffering from very congested platforms, the major remodelling of this part of London Bridge was only completed in 2018. (*Phil Tatt/Online Transport Archive*)

**Except for the viaduct** (left), everything in this view of London Bridge has changed. Among those heading for the station is a city gent with the once-familiar bowler and brolly. In stock from 1951 to 1976, RT3330 was one of over 3,000 RTs delivered without roof-boxes. (*Fred Ivey*)

**First introduced in 1930,** the Southern Railway's powerful 'Schools' Class were the last 4-4-0s to be built in Britain. Towards the end of its life, 30930 *Radley* speeds through Honor Oak Park with a down evening express. (*Fred Ivey*)

**Trolleybuses working the 1-in-9** grade on Anerley Hill needed special brakes. Replacing antiquated open top trams in 1935, these were short wheelbase B1 Leylands (64-93) with 60-seat BRCW bodies. Some time later, they were joined by B1s 489-493 displaced from Holloway. All were withdrawn by March 1959. (*Marcus Eavis/ Online Transport Archive*)

**Some intriguing forms of** transport were often hidden from the public unless you knew where to look. For example, Croydon 'A' Power Station used an overhead electric system for shunting coal wagons from 1925 to closure in 1973. Throughout, duties were in the hands of this single steeple-cab locomotive, built by English Electric, although a steam loco was available for when the electric required maintenance. (*Phil Tatt/Online Transport Archive*)

**Now pedestrianised, North End,** Croydon, remains a busy shopping street. On 1 September 1945, ex-Croydon Corporation 379 heads south towards Purley. At this time, routes 16/18 required some 80 trams in the morning peak. The 25 Croydon E/1s (375-339) dated from 1927 and had Hurst Nelson bodies and trucks. This was one of four rehabilitated in 1936. All had gone by March 1952. (*Harold Bennett*)

**Croydon was served by** two trolleybus routes, the longest of which was the 14-mile 630. In this view, 511, one of the Leyland D3s with BRCW bodies (494-553) delivered in 1936, is en route to Harlesden. Only a few D3s were still active when the replacement programme was implemented in 1959. (*Photographer unknown/Ian Stewart collection/Online Transport Archive*)

**Pristine 'Schools' Class 30926** *Repton* displays the four-disk head-code indicating it is in charge of the Royal Train as it heads through East Croydon bound for the races at Epsom in June 1962 with its royal party aboard. (*Charles Firminger/Online Transport Archive*)

**Although Croydon's heyday as** London's premier airport was in the interwar years, it was still used for a small amount of commercial activity in the 1950s. Against threatening skies, a Jersey Airlines de Havilland DH.114 Heron makes its final approach to the runway in 1957. (*Marcus Eavis/Online Transport Archive*)

**The 130 group of** Croydon-New Addington feeder routes were operated by Routemasters from the Autumn of 1964. The destination 'West Croydon' is white on blue and the upper deck band extends across the ventilator intakes at the front of RML2752, a change introduced later that year. (*John Herting/Online Transport Archive*)

**Coulsdon North is the** location for this picture of a six-car electric formation headed by 2-BIL 2091. These semi-fast units were introduced by the SR in 1935 and operated main line services to a variety of south coast destinations. (*Phil Tatt/Online Transport Archive*)

**The most prestigious SR** electric service was the 'Brighton Belle', the All-Pullman 10-coach train making the 50 mile trip from Victoria to Brighton in 60 minutes. Furore surrounded the decision to end the service in 1972 with luminaries such as Laurence Olivier bemoaning the loss of his breakfast kippers. This down working is seen near Norbury. (*Geoffrey Morant/Online Transport Archive*)

**In the London area,** Gatwick has always played second fiddle to Heathrow, although it was able to grow by attracting charter flights during the boom in package holidays. Scheduled airlines using Gatwick included British United Airways (BUA, rear left) and Dan-Air, whose DC3 Dakota G-AMSS has just arrived in this 1966 view. New in 1945, the aircraft was operated by Dan-Air between 1954 and 1968. (*Marcus Eavis/Online Transport Archive*)

**Despite its Scottish branding,** Caledonian Airways' main base was at Gatwick, where brand new BAC 1-11 G-AWWZ is seen in 1969. The company became British Caledonian the following year when it took over BUA and was absorbed into BA in 1988. (*Marcus Eavis/Online Transport Archive*)

**Overlooked by the Holmesdale** pub (since demolished), RLH52 passes along Park Lane East, Reigate, on route 430 in April 1962. This class had a single-piece destination display but at the front only. (*Roy Hobbs/Online Transport Archive*)

**A wealth of detail** is visible in this elevated overview of the station throat at Waterloo taken in the mid-1960s from the Shell Tower. A rebuilt Bulleid Pacific pulls out of platform 10 with an express, while BRCW Type 3s head rakes of coaches in adjacent platforms. In the foreground, two BR Class 4 2-6-4Ts simmer while waiting for their next duty, which will include empty stock workings to the sidings at Clapham Junction. (*Marcus Eavis/Online Transport Archive*)

**Looking east from the** same vantage point as overleaf, the line between Charing Cross and London Bridge can be seen snaking through Southwark. Many buildings survive today, including the distinctive St John's Church. (*Marcus Eavis/Online Transport Archive*)

**An anachronism amongst the** capital's underground railways was the Waterloo and City Line which, through its absorption by the London and South Western Railway in 1907, ultimately passed into BR ownership in 1948. The original units were replaced in 1940 by new SR stock which only saw daylight when brought up to ground level on a lift, as shown in this picture of newly-overhauled cars S84 and S52. The line transferred to LT ownership in 1994. (*Ray DeGroote/ Online Transport Archive*)

**Two generations of multiple** unit third-rail electric stock are seen at Waterloo in 1957. Nearest to the camera is 4-SUB 4517 on a Hampton Court service, composed of coaches which are of pre-Grouping design, the last of which operated in 1960. In the background, representing the newer order, is 4-EPB 5027, dating from 1953. (*Marcus Eavis/Online Transport Archive*)

**Owned by Albert Harling** Saloon Coaches of Lambeth and used to transport nurses to and from hospitals around Waterloo is former LT luxury coach RFW1, one of a small fleet of fifteen private hire vehicles purchased by LT in 1951. These AEC Regal IVs were fitted with elegant 39-seat 8ft wide ECW bodies. The last examples were withdrawn in 1964 with several being sold to Ceylon. (*M.J. Uden/Online Transport Archive*)

**During the final week** of tramway operation, E/1 578 approaches the junction of Blackfriars Road and Southwark Street. Dating from 1929/30, this is one of the 50 'Tunnel' or 'Reconstructed Subway' cars (552-601) which had new English Electric bodies but trucks and electrical equipment recycled from former single-deck subway cars. Although underpowered, most survived to the end. (*C. Carter/Online Transport Archive*)

*Opposite above:*
**In the post-war years,** BEA had a terminal at Waterloo from where express coaches ferried passengers to Heathrow. Seen in the late 1950s is one of 74 AEC Regal IVs delivered during 1953 with unusual deck-and-a-half Park Royal bodies with 37 seats and ample provision for luggage. The development of larger aircraft meant bigger vehicles were needed although one of these 4RF4s lasted until 1973. (*Julian Thompson/Online Transport Archive*)

**Fast and semi-fast trains** from Waterloo, such as that headed by BR-built Class 5 4-6-0 73065 in March 1967, would be getting up to speed by the time they passed through Vauxhall. Because of the full electrification of the South West main line through to Bournemouth later in the year, the loco would have just four months before withdrawal, when only 13 years old. (*Brian Faragher/ Online Transport Archive*)

**Freightliner was established by** BR as an attempt to revolutionise domestic freight movement in the 1960s. Trains of containers travelled by rail between terminals, with onward collection and delivery by road. Aboard a Guy Big J4 articulated lorry, a 30ft container is being loaded on Wandsworth Road in 1968. (*Harry Luff/ Online Transport Archive*)

**Since its opening in** 1932, Victoria Coach Station has handled millions of passengers on long-distance as well as shorter routes such as this Thames Valley service to Reading seen in 1960. To the rear of Bristol Lodekka 846 are coaches from famous operators Royal Blue and Black and White. *(Ian Stewart/Online Transport Archive)*

**The relatively cramped environment** of Victoria station means that photographs are not as common as other termini. The RCTS 'Wealden Limited' railtour of 14 August 1955 utilised seven different locomotives during the day. Departure from Victoria was behind ex-SE&CR E1 Class 4-4-0 31019 of 1908, which had been rebuilt from an earlier design in 1920. *(J.B.C. McCann/Online Transport Archive)*

**Many locomotives for Victoria's** non-electric services were provided by Stewarts Lane in Battersea, one of the largest motive power depots in Britain. One of the best known services in the country was the luxury 'Golden Arrow' boat train to Dover, for which Bullied 'Battle of Britain' Class 34085 *501 Squadron* is appropriately dressed. Awaiting more mundane duty is 'Merchant Navy' 35028 *Clan Line*. Both Pacifics still have their original streamlining. (*R.E. Vincent/The Transport Library*)

**The merging of lines** in the Stewarts Lane/ Clapham Junction area led to a complex arrangement of junctions and crossovers. Here W Class 2-6-4T 31917 is approaching Pouparts Junction with a mixed freight in 1962. Note the chimneys of Battersea Power Station in the background. (*Jim Oatway*)

**Drummond's M7 Class of** 0-4-4T locomotives of 1897-1911 were regular performers on suburban services and empty stock movements. 30241 enters the carriage sidings at Clapham Junction with an empty rake of coaches from Waterloo. The impressive 'A' signalbox, which straddled the tracks to the north of the station, was built in 1907 and closed in 1990, being demolished shortly afterwards. (*Fred Ivey*)

**Curving away from Clapham** Junction in the direction of Balham, and destined for Brighton, is 6-PUL set 3003. These twenty units were introduced by the Southern Railway in 1932 and featured one Pullman car in each six-car set, the one in 3003 being named *Grace*. The last 6-PULs were withdrawn in 1966. (*W.J. Wyse/LRTA (London Area)/Online Transport Archive*)

**Passing along Clapham Park** Road in November 1965 is RM1724. Starting in December 1962, the trunk 37 was one of the first to switch from RTs to Routemasters, with some 60 RM and RMLs needed on Saturdays. (*Alan Mortimer/Online Transport Archive*)

**In this incarnation, 3054** was a short-lived unit, designated 4-PUL. It was made up of three cars from a 4-RES (Portsmouth Line Express Restaurant) unit, but with the restaurant car replaced by a Pullman coach from a withdrawn 6-PUL, in this case *Clara*. It is seen in an eight-car formation near Wandsworth Common carrying a headcode for Eastbourne. (*Fred Ivey*)

153

**The flagship service on** the South West main line was the 'Bournemouth Belle' Pullman. In this view just south of Wimbledon, motive power is provided by rebuilt 'Merchant Navy' 35006 *Peninsular & Oriental S. N. Co.* From a group of 30 locos first introduced in 1941, this one has been rebuilt, losing its original streamlined casing. (*Julian Thompson/Online Transport Archive*)

**A pre-Grouping era 4-SUB** unit heads from Mitcham Junction towards Hackbridge, the headcode (L + 2 dots) indicating a London Bridge to Effingham Junction or Guildford service. In the background can be seen a signal post on the Croydon to Wimbledon line, which now forms part of Croydon Tramlink. (*Julian Thompson/Online Transport Archive*)

**The only place south** of the Thames where Tube trains can be seen in service above ground is on the approach to Morden at the end of the Northern Line. In 1969, a set of 1938 Tube Stock is completing its 17¼ mile underground journey across the city. (*John Herting/ Online Transport Archive*)

**The underground/ bus interchange at** Morden was nicknamed 'Daimlerland' when all 281 Utility Daimlers eventually ended up at nearby Merton and Sutton garages. Waiting to leave for Raynes Park in 1951 is D99, one of the batch with Brush bodies (D93-127) delivered in 1945. The last of these Utilities was sold in 1954. (*A.B. Cross collection*)

**Shortly before the inauguration** of the third rail electric service to Southampton and Bournemouth, a BRCW Type 3 diesel speeds through Surbiton with an eight-coach rake in 1966. The coaches comprise two 4-TC trailer sets which would soon be used with a 4-REP emu to provide twelve coach express electric trains between Waterloo and Bournemouth. This would mark the end of steam on the SR. (*Phil Tatt/Online Transport Archive*)

**Post-Nationalisation 4-SUB unit 4298** heads away from Shepperton with a Waterloo service on 5 February 1967, carrying the earliest version of BR blue livery, with small yellow warning panels. In the siding on the right is BR 2-6-4T 80145 on the LCGB's 'South West Suburban Railtour'. Virtually all signal boxes in the London area have now been closed and many demolished. (*Phil Tatt/Online Transport Archive*)

**For several decades, Walton-on-Thames** Motor Co. was the sole independent operating within the Central Area. Latterly three Duple-bodied Bedford OBs worked the mile-long link between the town and station. Just months after this view was taken in August 1969 all three were suddenly condemned. (*Martin Jenkins/Online Transport Archive*)

**Services on the former** London and South Western Railway route from Waterloo to Exeter, via Salisbury and Yeovil, were transferred from Southern to Western Region in the mid-1960s, resulting in 'Warship' class diesel-hydraulics becoming regular performers over the electrified lines into Waterloo. An unidentified member of the class approaches Walton-on-Thames shortly after the transfer of control. Note the gradual supplanting of coach liveries by BR blue and grey. (*Phil Tatt/Online Transport Archive*)

**Seen in 1969 at** Stoke D'Abernon on a short-working 462A is RF122, one of 175 RFs modernised during 1966/7 with twin headlights, improved lighting, single-piece windscreens plus a new livery featuring a wide green band. (*Mike Skeggs*)

**Leafy Woodham provides the** setting for this October 1968 view of RLH50 on a short-working 436A. This is one of 52 'green' RLHs assigned to Country Area garages between 1950 and 1952. Seventeen passed to London Country in 1970 with whom they had short lives, all being withdrawn by July. (*Alan Mortimer/Online Transport Archive*)

**The meandering 433 terminated** at its southern end close to Leith Hill in Coldharbour where GS42 is seen in April 1968. This was one of the last of this class to be withdrawn by LCBS in March 1972. (*Alan Mortimer/Online Transport Archive*)

**This view of STL1045** was taken in Guildford in 1951. It is from a small group of AEC Regents (STL1044-1055) dating from 1934. Originally assigned to Godstone garage, they had 48-seat low-bridge Weymann bodies with platform doors, crash gearboxes and powerful diesel engines suitable for steep hills. All were withdrawn by 1953. (*J. Law/Online Transport Archive*)

**This action-packed scene at** Onslow Street, Guildford, revives memories of the hustle and bustle of a 1960s bus station. On view on 9 May 1968 are RT4755 of 1954 and RLH25 of 1952. Note the range of adverts. Among the staff is a long-serving LT inspector. (*W. Ryan*)

**About to turn into** Onslow Street Bus Station on 9 May 1968 is Tillingbourne Valley No. 1. It is on route 448 which offered a rare example of a joint operation with LT although after 1964, Tillingbourne maintained the service with former GSs including GS1 which was a regular between 1963 and 1969. The arch on the left led into a large Pickford's yard and storage facility. (*W. Ryan*)

**Speeding along the A25** near Westcott in April 1968 is Country Area RF133 on the 412 Dorking to Sutton. (*Alan Mortimer/Online Transport Archive*)

**Parked at Crawley Bus** Station in 1967 are two Country Area veterans. RT1005 entered service in 1947 followed by RT3508 in 1951. Both survived with LCBS into the early 1970s. (*John Herting/Online Transport Archive*)

**Serving Littlehaven on the** route between Horsham and Roffey Corner is RT3693. Delivered with a Weymann body in 1953, it received a green Park Royal body in 1963 and was working from Crawley garage in the late 1960s. (*John Herting/Online Transport Archive*)

**BR Class 4 2-6-4** tank engine 80145 is seen at Kingston-upon-Thames on 5 February 1967, with the same railtour as seen on page 156. To the right is the former power station whilst on the river, a mix of commercial and pleasure craft are moored, allowing the sea cadets to get in some training. (*Phil Tatt/Online Transport Archive*)

**Passing under the trolleybus** wires at Twickenham in 1962, and on some sort of private working, is RMC4 (formerly CRL4 – Coach Routemaster Leyland). Seen shortly after being renumbered and painted into a short-lived light green livery, it differed from other Green Line Routemasters by having Leyland running units, an ECW body and full three-piece destination display. It passed to London Country in 1970 and was retained as an active heritage vehicle when withdrawn in 1979. It is now in private preservation. (*Tony Belton*)

**London's trolleybus story started** and ended at this former London United Tramways depot at Fulwell. They replaced trams on the LUT's local Kingston routes in 1931 and, two years later, the newly created LT then decided to scrap its huge fleet of inherited trams. However, the war intervened and the last tram to trolleybus conversion occurred in 1940 after which buses were preferred. With all trams gone by 1952, attention turned to the trolleybus network which was dismembered between 1959 and 1962. On May 8, the last day of service, No. 1, the first of the 60 original A1/A2 class AEC vehicles with UCC bodies, made a ceremonial journey from Fulwell to Kingston. (*Marcus Eavis/Online Transport Archive; Martin Jenkins/Online Transport Archive*)

**When the trams to** Tolworth were replaced, a new terminal loop was provided for the trolleybuses. This is one of the large fleet of chassisless L-class vehicles (1355-1529) delivered during 1939/40, all of which had Metro-Cammell bodies and Metrovick motors but were sub-divided according to brakes and controllers; for example, 1395 was an L/3 with Metrovick controllers. (*Jim Jordan/Online Transport Archive*)

**In the early 1950s,** Kingston garage was home to some veteran LGOC single-deckers built between 1929 and 1932, all originally with petrol engines. Representing the earliest of the T-class AEC Regals is T1. When withdrawn in 1951, it had an oil engine and renovated body. (*Alan B. Cross*)

**Passing Kingston Bus Station** in October 1960 is 1840, one of the Q1 trolleybuses (1765-1891) delivered in two batches between 1948 and 1953. These handsome vehicles had 8ft MCW bodies, BUT chassis and powerful 120hp motors and should have served the Kingston area for much longer but this all changed when the majority were sold to Spain in the early 60s. The bus station site has since been redeveloped. Both green and red RFs are seen on the 218 to Staines. (*Copyright Michael Wickham*)

**Always a magnet for** visitors, Hampton Court was served on summer Sundays by extensions of routes like the 14 and 27. Seen overtaking L3 trolleybus 1518 in 1961 is RTW48. It is one of 500 all-Leyland PD2s (RTW1-500) with 8ft wide bodies delivered during 1949/50. (*Tony Belton*)

**The Stevens family were** involved in the barge industry on the River Wey navigation since the early nineteenth century. In 1965, a train of their barges is seen making its way downstream at Hampton Court, headed by a small tug boat and with tillermen on the two rearmost barges. The bigger vessels would return with coal which was then sold through the family's coal merchants' business. (*J.G. Parkinson/ Online Transport Archive*)

**Windsor was served by** Green Line and Country Area buses. In 1965/6 100 lengthened 30ft versions of the Routemaster (RML2306-2355 and 2411-2460) were delivered to the Country Area. RML2435 is about to leave for Watford on the 335 – a route which hardly justified double-deckers – whilst RML2455 is on a relief Green Line 704. (*R.E. Vincent/The Transport Library*)

**Inter-regional freight transfers between** the LMR and SR took place near Willesden Junction at Old Oak Sidings, where 30494 is seen backing down onto a rake of wagons in May 1962. The loco was one of just four powerful Urie G16 4-8-0Ts introduced by the London and South Western Railway in 1921, which featured sloping front ends to the tanks to assist sighting. It is seen straddling the Grand Union Canal just six months before its withdrawal. (*Fred Ivey*)

**During 1956-63, LT purchased** 13 ex-GWR 0-6-0 Pannier tanks for use on their engineering trains, displacing some ageing ex-Metropolitan Railway locos. Seen in the late 1960s at West Kensington is L.99 with a train of sleepers from the nearby Lillee Bridge depot. These were the last steam locos to operate for LT – and indeed for anyone else in the capital – with the final example being withdrawn in 1971. (*John Herting/Online Transport Archive*)

**The short District Line** branch from Earl's Court to Kensington (Olympia) has generally only had an intermittent service, albeit enhanced when major events take place at the adjacent exhibition centre. In the late 1960s, a train of R Stock emerges onto the line. Seen in Lillie Bridge depot are a collection of battery electric locomotives, built from 1936 onwards. (*John Herting/Online Transport Archive*)

**Shortly before withdrawal, RT95** passes near Ravenscourt Park Station heading towards Hammersmith, whilst employed as one of the large, Chiswick-based driver training fleet. This is one of the 2RT2s (RT2-151) built between 1939 and 1942. As their Chiswick-built composite bodies proved less durable, most were withdrawn in 1955 although several survived in the training fleet. Also visible are a Scammell lorry and a Wall's delivery van. (*Tony Belton*)

*Opposite below:*
**After losing their passenger** service, some lines retained freight facilities for many years. In the case of the Hammersmith and Chiswick Branch from South Acton, passenger traffic ended in 1917 but the line was retained until 1965 to service a domestic coal facility. The former station was located the other side of the viaduct over which District and Piccadilly Line trains are approaching Stamford Brook station. This view dates from 20 April 1965. (*John Ryan*)

**A mixed set of** Q Stock leaves Gunnersbury in 1958 with a District Line service to Richmond. Note the detail differences between the various sub-categories of stock within the six-car formation. (*Julian Thompson/Online Transport Archive*)

**Turning into Gunnersbury Avenue,** Chiswick, is former RT1487 used by Permutit Water Softeners as a staff bus between 1956 and 1964. This view shows the non-standard five-bay Cravens body. (*Tony Belton*)

For many years, a large driver training fleet was based at the former LGOC works at Chiswick. In the first of two views taken in 1962, RT114 circumnavigates Chiswick roundabout. This is one of seven 'pre-war' RTs painted green for use during the mid-1950s on Hertford route 327 which involved a weight-restricted bridge. These early RTs differed from the post-war versions by having a downward sweep to the cab windows, seven ventilator apertures in the dash and a different destination display. Passing Chiswick Works entrance in the second view is RTL1262, one of eighteen RTLs painted green for Country Area work at Hatfield in 1959. Proving unpopular, they were swiftly moved on. (*Tony Belton*)

For many years, **Acton** Vale was served by trolleybus route 607 (Shepherd's Bush-Uxbridge). Regulars on this exceptionally heavy trunk route were the all-Leyland F1s (654-753) delivered in 1937 of which 712 is seen on 8 September 1960 just months before the route was converted. (*John Laker*)

**The grace of Brunel's** train shed at Paddington is evident in this 1965 view of one of the five 'Blue Pullman' sets introduced by BR in 1960 in a bid to attract more passengers onto the railway. This one is about to work the 4.50pm to Wolverhampton Low Level. In spite of the quality of the on-board facilities, they had all been withdrawn by 1973 and none survive today. (*Marcus Eavis/Online Transport Archive*)

*Opposite below:*

**For decades, Londoners relied** on public transport to access neighbourhood cinemas such as the Odeon at Acton Market, one of scores which have subsequently closed and been demolished. A significant snowfall on 31 December 1961 heralded some severe disruption over the next few days. For example, N1 1595 has been curtailed short of Hammersmith at Acton Market Place and is seen here in King Street, Acton, about to turn into the High Street. The vehicle is one of 90 AEC N1s (1555-1644) with BRCW bodies and Metrovick motors delivered during 1939/40. After many years at Bow depot they came west in 1959 and survived until January 1962. (*Tony Belton*)

**RT2601 passes the Load** of Hay pub on Praed Street in 1962 just months before the 36 group of routes were taken over by Routemasters. Carrying a Weymann body and standard three-section indicator display, this bus was in stock from 1951 to 1973. (*Tony Belton*)

*Opposite above:*
**On a chilly day** in January 1963, 'Hymek' D7039 prepares to pilot an unidentified 'Castle' away from Paddington on a down express. The last regular steam departure from Paddington was in 1965. (*Phil Tatt/Online Transport Archive*)

*Opposite below:*
**The GWR 'Castle' Class** of express 4-6-0s numbered 171, including locomotives rebuilt from other types. Emerging from the GWR works at Swindon in 1935, 5039 *Rhuddlan Castle* remained in stock until 1964. Overlooked by the massive GWR goods depot, it pauses just outside Paddington in 1958. (*Julian Thompson/Online Transport Archive*)

**Recalling the sheer volume** of parcels traffic once carried by rail, there were large sorting offices and warehouses across the network. Some of the contents on board W34W will transfer onto the underground Post Office Railway at Paddington. W34W is the last of thirty-four single unit railcars introduced by the GWR in 1934-42, two of which were designed for express parcels usage, the remainder being for passenger duties. The two parcels cars were withdrawn by 1962. (*R.E. Vincent/The Transport Library*)

**Locomotives and coaching stock** for Paddington were serviced at a complex of buildings and sidings at Old Oak Common, some two miles to the west. Running bunker first, a Collett 2-6-2T 61xx tank engine hauls a set of empty stock, wearing WR brown and cream livery, towards the depot in May 1962, whilst 'Castle' 7005 *Sir Edward Elgar* accelerates past on a down express. (*Fred Ivey*)

**Introduced in 1927, the** thirty 'Kings' were the most powerful passenger locos on the GWR and, in their heyday, these 4-6-0s handled the most important express trains out of Paddington. Although the class had been withdrawn by the end of 1962, 6018 *King Henry VI* was reinstated to haul the SLS 'Farewell to the Kings' tour of 28 April 1963. Here it pauses briefly at Southall. (*Phil Tatt/Online Transport Archive*)

Some of the 400 or so GWR general purpose 4-6-0 'Halls' and 'Granges' were regulars in the London area. 6848 *Toddington Grange* is at the head of a down express as it passes an inbound local at Southall. Note the single-unit GWR railcar stabled at the traction depot on the right. (*Julian Thompson/Online Transport Archive*)

The AEC works at Southall was always a good place to see new vehicles. Among the last 72-seaters to emerge were RML2664 and 2666 which had different registration numbers when they entered service in 1967. These marked the end of an era, as half-cab open platform double-deckers were now seen as too expensive and increasingly old-fashioned. The longer Routemasters had an additional small window on both decks. (*Fred Ivey*)

**'Standard' Tube Stock consisted** of units from a variety of manufacturers built between 1923 and 1934. Heading for Wood Green with a Piccadilly Line service, this train is departing from South Ealing in May 1955. The last of this stock ran in 1966, although a few sets were sold to BR and ran on the Isle of Wight until as late as 1992. (*Ray DeGroote/Online Transport Archive*)

**Many regretted the loss** of the distinctive red Underground livery. The first three sets of prototype 1956 Stock to have unpainted aluminium bodies also featured a range of modern features differentiating them from pre-war units. Their success led to the large orders of 1959 and 1962 Stock, from which they differed only in detail, such as the five headcode lights below the cab window. One of the prototypes is seen during a launch event at Northfields in 1956. (*Geoffrey Morant/Online Transport Archive*)

This 1962 line-up at Hounslow Bus Station features RT2408, RT691 and RT4366. Note the illuminated route number blind under the canopies. (*Tony Belton*)

**Until extended to Hatton** Cross in the mid-1970s, Piccadilly Line trains terminated at Hounslow West. Opened by the District Railway in 1884 and originally named Hounslow Barracks, these platforms were replaced by new underground ones as part of the extension work, with this site becoming the station car park. A train of 1959 Tube Stock is seen awaiting departure for Cockfosters. These units, and the almost identical 1962 Stock, were used at various times on the majority of Tube lines until their final withdrawal in 2000. (*Ron Copson/Online Transport Archive*)

**The observation terrace at** Heathrow gave enthusiasts unparalleled views of arrivals and departures. In this July 1963 scene, British Overseas Airways Corporation (BOAC) Comet 4 G-APDE is being pulled onto its stand prior to a long-haul flight. This was one of four of this type delivered to BOAC in September 1958 allowing it to introduce the first regular jet-powered Transatlantic service. Although BOAC went on to operate nineteen of the type, all had gone by 1969. (*Marcus Eavis/Online Transport Archive*)

**British Eagle was a** major independent airline until it went into liquidation in 1968. G-ATPJ was a BAC 1-11 new in 1966 and still in stock at the time of the company's closure. Note the ESSO Foden refuelling tanker with extra windows to aid visibility and the Thames Trader airside transfer vehicles. (*Marcus Eavis/Online Transport Archive*)

**British European Airways (BEA)** was the major customer for the distinctive Hawker Siddeley Trident, with its triple engines and T-tail. Three of the earliest variant are seen here at Heathrow in May 1966, the furthest one being G-ARPI. Sadly, this later crashed on 18 June 1972 at Staines shortly after take-off, with the deaths of all 118 people on board. It remains England's worst aviation accident. (*Marcus Eavis/Online Transport Archive*)

**A rare view of** RMF1254 photographed within the airport whilst on loan to BEA in the mid-1960s. Built a demonstrator in 1962, this front-entrance Routemaster was never operated by LT owing to union opposition. (*Marcus Eavis/Online Transport Archive*)

**Both state-owned airlines had** fleets of buses to move passengers to and from central London. During 1966/7, BEA purchased 65 forward-entrance 56-seat Routemasters (left). These were eventually sold to LT who had maintained and staffed them. The 88 associated luggage trailers were numbered N101-188. To convey passengers to and from its terminal at Victoria, BOAC purchased a fleet of MCW-bodied Leyland Atlanteans (above). Delivered during 1966, they had ample luggage space and luxury seats. The service ended in 1979 with the opening of improved rail connections. (*John Herting/Online Transport Archive*)

In May 1955, a set of P Stock pauses at Rayners Lane with a Metropolitan Line service for Uxbridge. O and P Stock, introduced from 1937 onwards, allowed the sub-surface lines to operate complete trains of modern looking cars for the first time. Upgraded in the 1950s, and redesignated CO/CP, the last examples ran in 1981. Extensions to the LT network in the 1930s and 1940s were characterised by Charles Holden's buildings in the modernist style. (*Ray DeGroote/Online Transport Archive*)

This view of RT491 at Northwood in September 1962 shows its offside route plate still in use. Withdrawn soon after, the bus went into store before being sold to Ceylon in 1964. (*Fred Ivey*)

**T750 stands at Uxbridge.** Delivered during 1946, the 14T14s (T719-768) had crash gearboxes and provincial-type, front-loading Weymann bodies with 'frowning fronts' to accommodate the LT-style destination box. Withdrawals took place between 1955 and 1958. *(Peter Grace, courtesy John Laker)*

**One of the few** lines to be discontinued in the London area was the short branch from West Drayton to Uxbridge Vine Street. Shortly before the end of passenger working in September 1962, a single unit railcar built by Pressed Steel in 1960 has just left Vine Street. Dwindling amounts of freight, especially domestic coal, were carried until 1964. *(Marcus Eavis/Online Transport Archive)*

**Waiting for passengers outside** the Vernon Arms at Hill End, Harefield, in 1967 is GS15, one of the class of 84 delivered during 1953/4. (*John Herting/Online Transport Archive*)

**Stopping at William IV** Crossroads in Langley in March 1966 is RF98, one from a batch of 39-seat Green Line coaches (RF26-288) which entered service during 1951/2. Note the Green Line fleet name and bullseye, side route boards and distinctive destination blinds which show it is on the long 705 Windsor to Sevenoaks. (*Alan Mortimer/Online Transport Archive*)

**The Willow Wren Canal** Carrying Co. Ltd. of Brentford operated extensively in the West London area. Fully sheeted, *Quail* leads another narrow boat out of the city along the Grand Junction Canal past Leybourne Wharf at West Drayton in 1957. (*Marcus Eavis/Online Transport Archive*)

**The Great Central Railway's** Marylebone Station was, in 1899, the last major terminal to open in London. However, it was in significant decline by the time LMS 'Black Five' 44570 departed with a down express, and suffered further with the closure of the bulk of the Great Central route in 1966. It has seen a resurgence in the years since rail privatisation. (*Roy Hobbs*)

**The first stop on** the Metropolitan Line out of Baker Street is Finchley Road, where there was cross-platform interchange with the Bakerloo Line (today the Jubilee). On the right on 26 July 1961 is a train composed of T Stock destined for Watford. These slam-door electric units were built in 1927-31 and were the mainstay of services to Watford and Rickmansworth until replaced by A Stock in 1961/2. On the left is a train of 1938 Stock on the Bakerloo service to Stanmore. (*John Ryan*)

**Nearing the end of** its journey along the Great Central, LMS 'Royal Scot' 46126 *Royal Army Service Corps* passes through West Hampstead in 1963. One of a class of 71 locos first introduced 1927, it was withdrawn shortly after this picture was taken. (*Fred Ivey*)

The majority of LT's steam fleet was shedded at Neasden and until the early 1960s included venerable machines ordered by the Metropolitan Railway. For example, L.52 was an 0-6-2 tank engine built by the Yorkshire Engine Company in 1901 for passenger services on the Aylesbury Line, whilst L.48 was an 0-4-4T constructed by Hawthorn Leslie in 1901. By this time, both had been relegated to works use and were scrapped by 1964. (*Harry Luff/Online Transport Archive; Ron Copson/Online Transport Archive*)

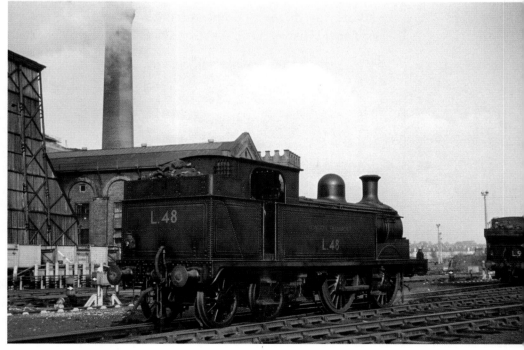

**No. 1** *John Lyon* was the first of the twenty Metropolitan-Vickers Bo-Bo electric locos built in 1922/3. It is seen at Neasden depot with a rake of hauled stock, led by coach 519 dating from 1900. Note the driver's compartment to facilitate push-pull operation on the Chesham Branch, and the adjacent 'Ladies Only' section. (*G.E. Lloyd Collection, courtesy Martin Jenkins/Online Transport Archive*)

**Parked at Parliament Hill** Fields on trolleybus replacement route 239 is RM514. Offside route numbers were dispensed with from 1963 and the title 'Routemaster' was no longer displayed above the fleet number after 1964. (*Julian Thompson/Online Transport Archive*)

**The morning mist at** Moor Park has not yet cleared as No. 16 *Oliver Goldsmith* heads an Aylesbury-bound service on 9 September 1961. The electric locomotive would be swapped for a BR steam engine at Rickmansworth for the final part of the journey. On the left, work is progressing on a major upgrade to allow expresses to run non-stop to and from Harrow-on-the-Hill. This involved a new four-track formation with the addition of two new platforms. (*John Ryan*)

**Prior to electrification in** September 1960, the Metropolitan Line branch from Chalfont and Latimer to Chesham was operated by BR steam locos for LT. Shortly before cessation of the steam service, and with third and fourth rails already installed, the push-pull train with post-war Ivatt 2-6-2T 41284 is at the branch terminus. (*Harry Luff/Online Transport Archive*)

**BR Fairburn 2-6-4 tank** 42281 pulls into Amersham with a city bound Metropolitan Line train on 6 August 1961. Note the pick-up shoe for current collection on the leading coach, which will come into use at Rickmansworth where the steam loco is replaced by an LT electric one. The service pattern changed in 1961 when LT services were curtailed at Amersham, with stations beyond being served solely by BR trains from Marylebone. (*John Ryan*)

So many of the once familiar sights seen in this book have all but disappeared including the great upstream docks as well as the trams, trolleybuses and half cab buses with conductors. Steam-hauled trains have been displaced by diesel and electric haulage and much rail-carried goods traffic has evaporated. The Underground remains a major artery for many travellers especially north of the Thames but it has lost most of its fascinating eccentricities. However, London will always remain a great source of fascination for the transport historian. Our last photograph is a glistening night shot of RTL737, westbound along Oxford Street. To the uninitiated, it looks like another half-cab double-decker but to the enthusiast, RTL551-1000 were of special interest because their all-metal MCCW bodies could not be exchanged with other bodies from the RT family at overhaul. (*Fred Ivey*)

*Opposite below:*
**This view highlights the** new arrangements on the Metropolitan Line just north of Amersham station on 26 May 1963. A BR Derby-built four-car DMU heads for Aylesbury whilst the LT A Stock train, built by Cravens of Sheffield, awaits its return journey to London having just terminated here. The much-loved A Stock units, dating from 1960-63, were finally withdrawn in 2012. (*Phil Tatt/Online Transport Archive*)

# Bibliography

During their research, the authors drew heavily on their own knowledge and experience, as well as those of many of the contributing photographers, whose personal insights into their images have brought the subject matter to life. Contemporary magazines, timetables and pamphlets were also consulted. This non-exhaustive list of books gives a sample of the range of publications used to verify facts and dates.

**BLACKER, Ken,** *RT: the story of a London Bus,* Capital Transport, 1979 (plus the author's equivalent books on other London bus types)

**BROWN, Joe,** *London Railway Atlas,* Ian Allan, 2006

**COLLINS, Paul,** *The Elephant Never Forgot,* Ian Allan, 2010

**DRYHURST, Michael,** *The London Trolleybus,* Dryhurst Publications, 1961

**GLAZIER, Ken,** *London Bus File 1946-49, 1950-54, 1955-62,* Capital Transport, 1998-99

**GREEN, Oliver and REED, John,** *The London Transport Golden Jubilee Book 1933-1983,* The Daily Telegraph, 1983

**JENKINS, Martin and STEWART, Ian**, *The Colours of Yesterday's Trams,* Capital Transport, 2012

**JOYCE, Jim,** *'Operation Tramaway'* Ian Allan, 1987

**LANE, Kevin,** *The Illustrated History of London Buses,* Ian Allan, 1997

**LONGWORTH, Hugh,** *British Railways Steam Locomotives 1948-1968,* Ian Allan, 2005

**LONGWORTH, Hugh,** *British Railways Electric Multiple Units to 1975,* Ian Allan, 2015

**OAKLEY, E.R. and HOLLAND, C.E.,** *London Transport Tramways 1933-1952,* The London Tramways History Group, 1998

**ROBERTSON, Kevin,** *The Last Days of Steam around London,* Alan Sutton Publishing, 1988

**RUSSELL, Michael,** *London Trolleybuses: a Colour Album,* Capital Transport, 2016

**TAYLOR, Hugh,** *London's Last Trams,* Adam Gordon, 2013

**WALLER, Peter,** *England's Maritime Heritage from the Air,* Historic England, 2017

Also many Ian Allan ABC railway, bus, aviation and ocean shipping books, various fleet history publications of the PSV Circle, and Regional Handbooks of the Industrial Railway Society.

Many websites provided up-to-date material, most notably Ian's Bus Stop (www.countrybus.org) which provided comprehensive details of most vehicles featured.

And finally, with reference to Charles's earliest London memories in the introduction:

**McCULLOCH, Derek,** *In the train with Uncle Mac,* Wills and Hepworth ('Ladybird'), 1955

**ŠAŠEK, Miroslav,** *This is London,* W.H. Allen, 1959

*Martin Jenkins*
*Walton-on-Thames*

*Charles Roberts*
*Upton, Wirral*

*July 2018*